The Stream Invites Us to Follow

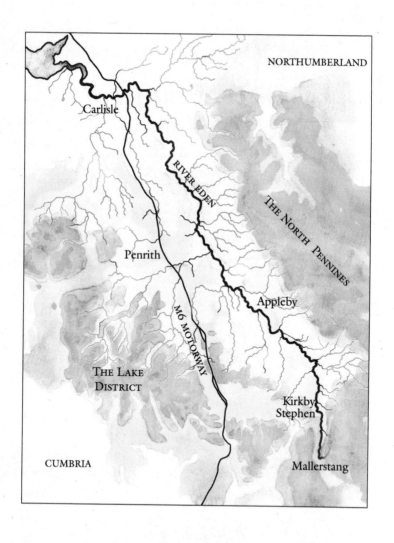

NORTHUMBERLAND

Carlisle

RIVER EDEN

THE NORTH PENNINES

Penrith

M6 MOTORWAY

Appleby

THE LAKE
DISTRICT

Kirkby
Stephen

CUMBRIA

Mallerstang

The Stream Invites
Us to Follow

Exploring the Eden
from Source to Sea

Dick Capel

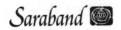

Published by Saraband
Digital World Centre,
1 Lowry Plaza,
The Quays, Salford, M50 3UB

ISBN: 9781912235841
ebook: 9781912235858

*The author and publisher make no claim that the walking routes
described here are safe or that access is allowed other than where
public rights of way are marked on the current Ordnance Survey
map. The banks of the Eden and its tributaries are often undermined
and eroded during extreme weather and floods. This presents hazards
for walkers – even those familiar with the area. Anyone wishing to
recreate stages of the author's route does so at their own risk.*

Printed and bound in Great Britain by Clays Ltd, Elcograf S.p.A.

10   9   8   7   6   5   4   3   2   1

For Oonagh

Contents

One

Mallerstang

Eventually, all things merge into one and a river runs through it. The river was cut by the World's great flood and runs over rocks from the basement of time.

Norman Maclean, *A River Runs Through It*

In the south-eastern corner of Cumbria, two springs of crystal-clear water called Red Gill and Slate Gutter ooze out of Black Fell Moss, a remote bog high up on the eastern side of the spectacular Mallerstang valley. Liberated from the saturated, clinging peat, they scamper over the brow of the hill and converge to form Hell Gill Beck, the boisterous adolescent stream that runs south-west down into the valley bottom and swings abruptly north to become the River Eden.

For many years, as the curlews returned to greet the arrival of spring with their plaintive, bubbling cry, I have visited the source of the River Eden; a personal annual pilgrimage after the long, cold paralysis of winter to celebrate both the awakening of the new year and the embryonic rise of the river. On one late-March visit, it didn't feel at all like spring up there; lines of thick snow lay across the moor, and grey sheets of ice glazed the pools of water skulking inside its dark peat hollows. The bleak fell was still chillingly comatose under a leaden sky, frozen in the tenacious grip of winter's malevolent spell. There was no sound of the curlew that had earlier greeted my arrival in the valley below, and I listened in vain for skylarks or meadow pipits or the distant

1

fluting of golden plovers. The morose moor was unrelentingly silent, and a screen of smoke rising on the horizon, where game-keepers were burning the heather, partially concealed the stark outline of Ingleborough, lending emphasis to the melancholy of a lost wilderness.

I didn't stay long. My pilgrimage on that occasion was also the start of a journey along the entire length of the River Eden, which had to begin at the top of the hill known as Hugh Seat. There, at a height of 689 metres above the valley bottom, I could attain a real sense of the watershed where, as old documents describe it, 'Heaven water deals' and 'Heaven water divides'. With Mallerstang Edge to the east and Wild Boar Fell to the west, virtually identical heights of just over 700 metres, Mallerstang belongs, geologically, to the limestone country of the Yorkshire Dales. Dominated by horizontal layers of carboniferous limestone, capped with gritstone escarpments, it represents more than 350 million years of geological history. Derived from sediment deposited and compressed by shallow tropical seas and primeval rivers, lifted by tumultuous upheavals in the Earth's crust, they were cut into shape by the interminable passage of Ice Age glaciers and the melting, manic water in their wake.

Surrounded by that vast ancient landscape, I always feel acutely aware of the fleeting and minuscule time span of human history; a mere two million years. A very small stone cairn on top of Hugh Seat, inscribed faintly with the initials AP and the date 1664, puts this neatly into perspective. The cairn is Lady's Pillar, erected at the request of an extraordinary seventeenth-century landowner called Lady Anne Clifford, the Countess of Pembroke, who owned vast tracts of old Westmorland stretching between Mallerstang and Penrith. It marks the source of the river and commemorates her notorious predecessor, the Norman knight

Sir Hugh de Morville, who owned the same estates five hundred years earlier and was one of the four knights who murdered Thomas Becket, the Archbishop of Canterbury.

My plan was to travel the route in stages, short sections at a time, sometimes walking, sometimes by car, over the course of the proceeding seasons. I descended from Hugh Seat feeling disappointed that there were no stirrings of spring at the source of the river. But I still had the warmer embrace of the green valley below to look forward to, with its promise of skydiving lapwing, their sharp *pee-wit* call complementing the curlews' lugubrious refrain, and perhaps the sight of a few early spring flowers on sheltered grassy banks.

As I stumbled down the hill a pair of grouse hurtled out of the drab, brittle heather in front of me, whirring and gliding, a feather's breadth from the ground, on stubborn, stubby wings and seemingly mocking my retreat from the moor with their call to *go bak, bak, bak, bak*. At that moment one of the frozen pools erupted in a turmoil of spluttering, spouting silver bubbles, like a cauldron of boiling water. For a split second I thought I'd encountered a geyser of hot spring water bursting through the peat from the subterranean depths below Black Fell Moss. Drawing closer, I realised it was frogs; a tumultuous tangle of copulating frogs rising to the surface in a frenzied orgy of vernal ecstasy. Perhaps the grouse were right and I'd been too hastily dismissive of the desolate moor. In being so preoccupied with watching and listening for manifestations of spring in the air I'd been ignoring the ground beneath my feet.

It was perfect. Water was going to be my regular companion as I travelled along the length of the river, and here was an entirely unexpected aquatic affirmation of renewal that lifted my spirits, filling me with an almost delirious surge of anticipation at the commencement of my journey. The now confident stream was gathering momentum, channelling its way along the bottom of the steep-sided gully it had gouged out over thousands of years. Its eroded banks are jagged with crumbling landslips and strewn with big broken slabs of stone that are testament to the water's more aggressive progress and continuing excavations after heavy rain. Scrambling down the slope into the gill, shut off from the wider landscape, I felt a profound sense of intimacy with the river. Then, as I walked along its cloistered banks, the sound of rushing water filled the air like a chorus of voices chanting a mesmeric mantra from, in Norman Maclean's words, the "basement of time".

I arrived in Cumbria in 1982 to work as an area warden for the Yorkshire Dales National Park in its north-west region and lived for the first twenty-five years in a sixteenth-century cottage at Fell End, on the other side of Wild Boar Fell. I lived there for eight years before I became properly acquainted with the River Eden, because my life, at that time, was being entirely shaped by the work I was doing in the upper catchment areas of both the River Ure in Wensleydale and the River Lune in Garsdale, Dentdale and the area around Sedbergh.

It wasn't until I moved jobs in 1991 and went to work for East Cumbria Countryside Project (ECCP) that I switched catchments and discovered the Eden Valley with its river and tributaries. It was a revelation in more ways than one. I had become disenchanted with my job in the National Park. At first it seemed like a dream come true; for years I'd seen the national park concept as a 'green-print' of an ecologically sustainable future for the countryside as a whole – a partnership between local government and local residents, particularly the farming community, all working together to manage a productive rural economy in harmony with maintaining a beautiful landscape and a rich diversity of wildlife.

Or so I thought! Instead there was conflict and resentment at every turn. The farmers hated the National Park, and the National Park Authority maintained an aloof and condescending attitude to the farmers. Local residents, generally, grappled with inconsistent and intransigent planning restrictions. Visitor management was outmoded and still based on the American model of a national park, which, in my view, was entirely inappropriate and endlessly confusing to the public. In the UK they are not parks, nor are they nationally owned as they are in the USA. The vast majority of the farms are privately owned or tenanted by farmers who feel that they are themselves an integral part of the land they farm. They are inherently territorial, and I came to feel sympathetic to their point of view. A senior member of staff told me, in no uncertain terms, that I was becoming "too friendly with the farmers", and yet I truly believed that the essence of my role was to win the trust of the farmers and recruit their support in a grand vision that would benefit everyone. As he saw it, however, I was consorting with the enemy.

Thankfully most of the national park authorities have changed considerably since those early days and adopted a much more enlightened and sensitive attitude toward the farming community. Their planning procedures too are now substantially more conciliatory, creative and facilitating. But they are still called national parks.

* * *

And so I slithered and climbed down Hell Gill's dim, glistening insides, through a succession of cold baths, in one long primal scream.

Roger Deakin, *Waterlog*

Hell Gill divides Cumbria from Yorkshire and was the northern boundary of the Yorkshire Dales National Park until 2015 when the park was extended further north to include an extra 417 square kilometres in Cumbria, now called the Westmorland Dales. The River Ure starts its journey in the opposite direction just a short distance from here on the Yorkshire side.

The nascent River Eden snakes its way across level ground before plunging into the narrow, hidden cavity of Hell Gill, the limestone gorge that gives the beck its name. More than a thousand years ago Mallerstang was occupied by Viking farmers, so Hell Gill may well have been Hel's Gill, an entrance to the Viking underworld of the dead, which in Norse mythology was called Hel and ruled over by a goddess who was also named Hel. The Viking Hel was a more benign place than the Christian version of Hell, but, even so, it must have been a depressing prospect for the local Vikings to have its entrance on their patch, not to mention a soul-destroying job for their goddess.

Hell Gill is 30 metres deep and 365 metres long, yet, in places, little more than a metre wide. Most of the time it tumbles gently in a series of hidden waterfalls and pools. Braver people than me venture down there in the drier summer months, coming in from the top end, sliding and slipping from pool to pool in the half light and emerging at the bottom to dry themselves on exposed rocky ledges in the brightness and warmth of the sun. In spate the beck fills the ravine with a raging, plunging, crashing torrent. In his book *Waterlog*, the late Roger Deakin describes how he attempted to scramble down the Gill in more running water than was reasonably safe and halfway down found himself beneath an overhanging rock, staring into a terrifying "gothic emptiness". Sensibly, he retreated and climbed back to the top, despite the full strength of the water being against him. I was happy to give the experience a miss and, skirting to one side, came down onto the wide green track still known as Lady Anne's Highway.

The Highway was an important trading route for hundreds of years and once the only way through the valley. It was almost certainly frequented by highway robbers, and legend has it that during a violent storm that had destroyed the bridge across Hell Gill, the infamous highwayman Dick Turpin escaped the clutches of pursuing policemen by leaping across the gorge on his horse, Black Bess. The legend might have some basis in fact, although it is more likely to have been a local highwayman called Ned Ward, who was active in the eighteenth century, than Dick Turpin. Ned was a native of the dale who, with his accomplice Broderick, apparently confined his criminal endeavours to robbing wealthy off-comers and leaving local inhabitants well alone. This approach, perhaps an interesting example of early hill farm diversification in the absence of agricultural subsidies, gave the villains some protection from the law. Eventually, though, one stormy night, the police arrived with warrants for their arrest. Having successfully apprehended Broderick, they failed to catch Ned, who broke through the thatched roof of his cottage and galloped off on one of the constables' horses. He may or may not have jumped over the bridgeless gorge, but he did escape and, according to accounts at the time, eventually settled in the Newcastle area to become a coal miner. According to Alfred Noyes, the hero of his poem 'The Highwayman' "rode with a jewelled twinkle / His pistol butts a-twinkle." I don't suppose that was the case with Ned, but I like to think he had a twinkle in his eyes.

* * *

From Hell Gill Bridge, or Devil's Bridge as it is sometimes known, the beck meanders through several fields and then, close to where it turns north at the bottom of the valley, pours over a steep cliff in a waterfall called Hell Gill Force. Depending on recent rain levels, the waterfall varies in size from a timorous trickle to a demonic deluge. I am always amazed at how quickly rivers rise after a day or two of heavy rain.

The ground along the horizon on the opposite side of the valley, known as The Nab, just left of Wild Boar Fell's pointed summit, bristles with a row of tall thin cairns that are like teeth in a crocodile's jaw. Wild Boar Fell was presumably a good place to find wild boar, once upon a time, before they became extinct in this country. Sir Richard Musgrave, a fifteenth-century knight who lived in Kirkby Stephen, reputedly killed the last one. As if to prove this, a boar's tusk was found years ago in his tomb in Kirkby Stephen's church. Perhaps the cairns were put up by him, like notches on a trophy hunter's gun, to keep a tally of all the wild boar he'd slaughtered.

Lady Anne's Highway crosses rougher ground going south to Cotter Riggs, where it joins what is now the A64 to Hawes, but I was heading north along a flat section of the track that runs parallel with the infant northbound River Eden in the valley below. The wide, straight path here has the feel of a classic green road: the grass grows in thin soil over flat slabs of limestone pavement and is kept cropped short by the incessant nibbling of Swaledale sheep.

Lady Anne Clifford travelled regularly along this route on arduous journeys between her castle at Skipton and the four castles she owned in Westmorland. It was very different in her day. Sitting precariously in a horse litter – rather like a sedan chair supported by long poles slung between two horses at the front and rear – she was always accompanied by an army of noisy companions and servants on horseback and in numerous creaking carriages with a cart, pulled by oxen, carrying her heavy bed. The road would have been much more rutted and slippery with mud, making progress agonisingly slow for such a bizarrely attired procession in all their pretentious cavalier splendour.

Passenger trains along the Settle to Carlisle railway, on the opposite side of the valley, now provide a more comfortable way to travel, but, when the line was being constructed from 1869 to 1875, between Dent and Kirkby Stephen, a workforce of some six thousand navvies suffered appalling hardship and deprivation. It's difficult to imagine the sprawling shanty towns built to accommodate the workers and their families and the devastating impact they had on the local farming community in what had previously been, and is now again, such a remote and tranquil valley.

The walk along this elevated track is always special, but never more so than on that particular euphoric morning. Patches of blue sky had emerged by then, and the sun was filtering through the dispersing clouds in columns of golden dust. Curlews and several pairs of lapwing, so conspicuous by their absence on the high fells, cavorted above my head, consolidating their recent arrival in the dale with amicable whoops. The very same resonant calls had greeted the Viking farmers, the Norman knight Sir Hugh de Morville, Lady Anne Clifford, the highwayman Ned Ward and the thousands of navvies building the railway at the start of all their individual springs.

Two

Eden Benchmarks

My pace quickened with the imminent prospect of reaching the vantage point ahead where, on a clear day, the upper Eden Valley comes into view. It is also the place where the sculpture *Water Cut* is sited, and it would be false modesty to deny that my exhilaration was partly because it was me who put it there.

Water Cut is one of ten stone sculptures I commissioned, called Eden Benchmarks, whilst working for ECCP. Each by a different artist and sited at locations dispersed along the entire length of the River Eden, they were installed to celebrate the new millennium in 2000. The artists were selected by community representatives and worked in residence for six weeks in local workshops. This enabled them to formulate their ideas in relation to the sites and discuss them with local residents, including schoolchildren, who were encouraged to visit and see the sculptures taking shape.

Collectively the sculptures underline our visual and emotional appreciation of the river in a way that enhances a sense of place at each different location. My brief to the artists was that the Eden Benchmark sculptures should be, first and foremost, sculpture for sculpture's sake. Their function as seats would be secondary to their aesthetic value in harmony with the landscape.

Water Cut stands on the hill like a huge milestone with a curvaceous gash cut vertically down its middle, describing the symbolic shape of a river in the sky and providing a window onto the real river in the valley below. Made with Salterwath Limestone by the Scottish sculptor Mary Bourne, it was erected in 1997. Its principal theme is the power of the river cutting through the rocky landscape over aeons of time, but it is also intended to evoke a feeling of our individual human journeys through the landscape and, perhaps more profoundly, our journeys through life. Dizzy with this mix of philosophical and emotional thinking, I was glad to sit down on its flat polished base. For all its deeper meanings, *Water Cut* provides a majestic throne, commensurate with the stunning view, for sitting still and contemplating the surrounding scenery. As the Zen Buddhist master once said: "Don't just do something – sit there!"

Mary Bourne was born in Brighton but brought up in Aberdeen. She graduated from Edinburgh College of Art in 1986 and now lives in the Scottish Highlands. I first became aware of her work in 1990, at the beginning of her career, when she was an Artist in Residence at Irvine New Town. During a three-year period, she created an impressive collection of stone sculptures sited around the town. When I first devised the proposal for Eden Benchmarks, I searched for professional sculptors not only on the basis of their creativity but, most importantly, on their ability to carve stone. Mary stood out as a consummate artist and a wonderful stone carver. She describes her artistic practice as "striving to encapsulate intensities of feeling. The time consuming and arduous technique of hand carving stone dictates simplification and concentration on the essential. In time I arrive at images which are crystallisations of my subjective experience of landscape."

Local farmer Steve Alderson and his son Kevin installed *Water Cut* for us. Mary had carved the massive blocks of stone in one of Steve's outbuildings and gained his increasing respect with her sheer daily hard work, perseverance and skill. He and Kevin transported the three pieces of the sculpture on tractor-drawn trailers and, with enthusiastic efficiency, assembled it on site.

Once the base was secured to a concrete foundation, they low-ered the two vertical pieces onto it and fixed them with steel pins. They completed the operation over two days, with minimal equipment and fuss, utilising the resourceful ingenuity and good humour that is so characteristic of Cumbrian farmers.

In the months leading up to the installation I was involved in numerous meetings with local people, the local author-ity and, most importantly, the landowner concerned. The site is on Mallerstang Common, which was then the responsibility of the late Giles Thompson, who was Lord of the Manor and lived at nearby Hanging Lund. I'd approached him with some trepidation as he was an eccentric and formidable character with conservative and traditional opinions. I didn't expect him to be sympathetic to my proposal that we erect a 'modern' sculpture on such a prominent part of his estate. In the event, though, he was supportive.

The local authority also approved of the project and assured me that there would be no need to seek formal planning permis-sion, based on my description of sculptures that would function as seats. This, of course, had implied they would all be low hori-zontal objects and therefore exempt from planning restrictions relating to structures above a certain height. Consequently, as I drove away along the bottom of the valley, on the evening we finished installing *Water Cut*, I was rather worried when I looked back up the hill and realised how clearly visible it is from that distance, albeit only a small protuberance on the horizon. I lay awake that night fretting that there might be repercussions from the Planning Department, but to my great relief nothing was ever said to suggest disapproval. On the contrary, photo-graphs of *Water Cut* are regularly featured in Eden District Council's tourism brochures and it is much acclaimed by locals and visitors alike.

Local residents were virtually unanimous in their support, and an intrepid group of them, with several dogs and a pony, assembled on a rainy, windy day to watch Lord Inglewood and I attempting to drape a length of white net curtain over the sculpture to prepare for a formal unveiling. The wind was so fierce, however, that it snatched the veil up into the air with Lord Inglewood holding valiantly to one end. The sedate unveiling we'd anticipated was transformed into a triumphant and exhilarating flag-flapping, banner-billowing, gale-force celebration instead. Mallerstang just wasn't in the mood, that day, for a sedate ceremony.

The meaning of the name Mallerstang is uncertain but commonly thought to derive from a variant spelling, 'mallardstank', meaning 'a duck-inhabited marsh'. According to better-informed opinion, however, it originates from a combination of *moelfre*, a Celtic word meaning 'bare hill', and *stong*, Norse for 'landmark'. We didn't know this at the outset. It could well be a reference to the cairns near the top of Wild Boar Fell, but *Water Cut* does provide an iconic sculptural *stong* to commemorate our particular time in history at the head of the Eden Valley. It certainly represented a culminating moment for me, in the context of a liberating and regenerating phase of my life.

I started my job as a Countryside Project Officer with ECCP in 1992. At that time it was led by an unusually enlightened and forward-thinking young woman called Isobel Dunn, who tragically died of cancer a year or so after I joined. She left behind a group of independent-thinking individuals who shared a collective commitment, drive and determination to deliver a dynamic and innovative countryside management service that was second to none. Despite its continuing and celebrated success over the ensuing years, ECCP was closed down in March 2009 following a withdrawal of funding by its local authority partners, Cumbria County Council, Eden District Council and Carlisle City Council.

Since its original inception in 1976, ECCP had established a reputation for an inventive approach to helping people enjoy the countryside. A degree of freedom was encouraged to empower its staff to try out new and unconventional ideas. Mine was the idea of using the arts as a vehicle for exploring emotional interactions with the environment. I had long admired the organisation Common Ground, which pioneered the concept of environmentalists and artists working together to enhance understanding and enjoyment of the natural world. I was inspired by a sculpture project they initiated in Dorset called New Milestones and I had dreamt that one day I might be given the chance to do something similar. Joining ECCP and the timely announcement by the Arts Council that 1996 was to be designated Visual Arts Year serendipitously gave me that chance, and I put together my plan for Eden Benchmarks.

Over the course of the four years it took to complete the collection I was riding on the crests of waves of good fortune and goodwill. Northern Arts was supportive, as were Eden Arts and Eden District Council. As each sculpture was installed and featured in the local press and on television, the public response was heart-warming.

On a personal level, making it all happen was a thrilling adventure. Working closely with the artists concerned, liaising with locals in choosing locations, negotiating with the landowners, visiting quarries with the artists to select lumps of raw stone, organising contractors to deliver the stone to the artists' workshops and then installing the finished sculptures gave me a sense of achievement on a scale I'd never experienced before.

Yet it was everybody else involved who did all the real work. The sculptors, without exception, were such nice people. They worked incredibly hard in the short time they were allotted, with a passionate and awesome creativity. Landowners astounded me with their generous co-operation, quarrymen with their kindness and patience and contractors with their easygoing and good-humoured ingenuity and expertise. Everything seemed to just fall into place. I was part of a winning team.

Three

The Road to Pendragon Castle

I have seen the walls of Pendragon, but they were desolate....
The fox looked from the windows and the rank grass of the wall
waved round his head. Desolate is the dwelling of Pembroke;
silence is in the house of her fathers.

Fawcett Hunter of Fell End, Ravenstonedale, 1797

From *Water Cut,* the panoramic vista of the Pennines stretches across the horizon with only a partial view of the Eden Valley plateau through a narrow gap at the northern end of the dale. The flat summit of Cross Fell, 893 metres high, and Great Dun Fell with its 'giant golf ball' radar station dominate the scene over to the left. Ranging across to the right is the expanse of fell owned by the Ministry of Defence, one of the biggest army training areas in the UK.

As I stood up to resume my walk a female kestrel swooped down in front of me, settling into a pocket of air with her quivering pointed wings outstretched, poised like a prima ballerina. She hung there for some minutes, huge eyes fixed upon a millimetre of turf 10 metres below. Then, dropping with ballistic accuracy to the ground, she lay briefly spread-eagled in the tufted sedge before springing into flight and speeding away with a vole clenched in her talons. I love hawks. I always feel so privileged when I see them, and sad when I think how the persecution they have suffered in the past continues to this day, despite legislation that is supposed to give all hawks absolute legal protection.

Of all the birds of prey, sparrowhawks are my favourite. J.A. Baker described them in his seminal book *The Peregrine*, published in 1967, as always being near him in the dusk "like something I meant to say but could never quite remember. Their narrow heads glared blindly through my sleep. I pursued them for many summers, but they were hard to find and harder to see, being so few and so wary. They lived a fugitive, guerrilla life. In all the overgrown neglected places the frail bones of generations of sparrowhawks are sifting down now into the deep humus of the woods. They were a banished race of beautiful barbarians and when they died, they could not be replaced".

Sparrowhawks were brought to the brink of extinction in the 1960s, along with peregrine falcons, by the indiscriminate use of organochlorine pesticides in agriculture. Just in the nick of time the government banned their use, and populations of both of these truly magnificent predators have since gradually recovered.

Whereas kestrels seem almost oblivious to human company and are often seen hovering above motorway and roadside verges, sparrowhawks are clandestine hunters. They are noble savages, ever vigilant, concealing themselves in woods and hedges and looking out at us with angry yellow eyes. I think that's why I like them so much. They are creatures of the original 'wildwood'. Only when they think we're not watching do they slip out of their hiding places in low gliding forays, twisting and turning, then pouncing on their prey with a swashbuckling, feather-busting flourish. Despite some continuing persecution, their population levels for the moment remain fairly stable. Long-term studies indicate, however, that significant numbers of them are now starving to death due to a scarcity of the smaller birds they eat. I often hear people blaming sparrowhawks for the reduction of these smaller birds when, in fact, it is modern farming methods that have led to their decline. Optimum populations of small birds are well able to withstand sparrowhawk predation on farmland where their shared habitats are responsibly conserved.

Certain species, like hen harriers, are still being persecuted in the remote open uplands they inhabit and are poisoned and trapped on grouse moors with sickening regularity throughout the north of England and most of Scotland. If it wasn't for this illegal slaughter, there would be several hundred breeding pairs across England, instead of which only one or two pairs have nested successfully in recent years. The success of breeding peregrine falcons has also been found in recent surveys to be 50 per cent lower on grouse moors than elsewhere. Little seems to have changed since the Victorian era. Detecting and gathering evidence of this criminal activity is notoriously difficult. Even when there is a successful prosecution, the perpetrator of the crime is invariably a gamekeeper who takes the blame whilst his affluent, hypocritical employer, who gives him his orders and probably pays the fines, remains beyond the reach of the law.

The trouble with walking is that it stimulates a lot of thinking, which isn't always conducive to enjoying the actual walk. I like the Buddhist idea of walking meditation, which advocates concentrating mindfully on the here and now and on the contact we feel between the soles of our feet and the ground. We should let our feet do more of the thinking. The route goes downhill from *Water Cut* on a track that only a few years ago was deeply rutted, potholed and permanently running with water. Its surface was dramatically improved and culverts were installed a few years ago when it became part of the officially designated Pennine Bridleway. Because of its historic status as a road, it is officially designated as a Byway Open to All Traffic. Those in the know call them BOATS. In common with most walkers, I tend to disapprove of the increasing numbers of people who exploit what I regard as an illogical legal loophole. Our world is already overwhelmed by the internal combustion engine, with CO_2 emissions polluting our skies as well as the air we breathe. The noise of traffic dominates our everyday lives along with the relentless proliferation of roads and motorways to accommodate it. So why must we suffer the intrusion of off-road motor vehicles shattering our peace in quiet, remote parts of our rural environment?

At the instant I had that thought, a vehicle appeared at the bottom of the hill. I watched as it lumbered towards me, disappearing then reappearing as its driver negotiated the sharp bends and dipped into the hollows to cross the traversing becks. So much for letting my feet do the thinking. As it drew nearer, I tried to regain my composure and suppress my annoyance. At least, I reasoned with myself, it was just the one vehicle. The large four-wheel-drive, shiny black, chrome-embellished, tank-proportioned truck contained a smiling middle-aged couple who were enjoying themselves enormously and who greeted me with friendly waves. As they passed I almost regretted the meanness of my smile. Surely I have far worse things to worry about.

Nonetheless, on a purely practical level, the damage these vehicles cause is considerable. They often travel in convoys, their drivers apparently motivated by the eagerly anticipated likelihood that some of them will get stuck up to their axles in mud. This provides them with an opportunity to satisfy what appears to be a quasi-militaristic compulsion to test the capabilities of their all-terrain vehicles to the limit, not to mention their own somewhat dubious driving skills and their enthusiastic over-reliance on using a winch when they get stuck. The deep ruts and ridges they cause are hazardous to walkers and horse riders, particularly horse riders (and this is a bridleway), yet they have no obligation to pay for repair of the damage they leave in their wake.

The valley at the base of Wild Boar Fell, beneath the railway line, is a pleasing mix of farmsteads, walled fields and scrubby woodland. There is a public footpath alongside the river there, unlike elsewhere in Mallerstang. Public Rights of Way often follow what seem to us irrational routes because they originate from a time when there were no motor vehicles. Local residents walked or travelled on horseback everywhere. Consequently, most of the paths in Mallerstang follow the shortest routes connecting the houses with churches, chapels and schools. The fields containing the barns are, or were, hay meadows. The barns were built with two floor levels so that hay cut in the summer could be stored upstairs and fed directly to cattle, which were housed downstairs, in the winter. Since the advent of the tractor, farming activities have become more centralised so most of the field barns, such a characteristic component of the traditional dales landscape, have become obsolete and are gradually becoming derelict, many disappearing.

Looking up at the lofty limestone escarpment of Mallerstang Edge reminds me of the dramatic scenery in 'cowboys and Indians' films, and I half expect to see a row of Apache warriors on horseback staring down at me with disdain. It is much more likely, of course, they would be Viking ghosts. The area surrounding the bottom of Lady Anne's Way is called Boggle Green. *Boggle* is a Celtic or Norse word for a ghost, so if ever I do see a line of horsemen up there, it will probably be Viking zombies riding spectral steeds to the ghoulish nether regions of Hell Gill.

* * *

It was almost a relief to emerge on the road and walk along to Outhgill, a hamlet of seven or eight houses. At one time they included a public house, which would have provided me with some welcome refreshment, but it closed a long time ago. A blacksmith, a community hall, a shop, post office and school are also long gone. The little church was built in the fourteenth century and lay in ruins for many years until the ubiquitous Lady Anne Clifford came along and restored it.

A replica of a stone pillar called the Jew Stone stands on the village green where it was erected in 1989. The original pillar was installed by William Mounsey near the source of the River Eden in 1850 and destroyed by vandals twenty years later. Mounsey lived north of Carlisle, at Castletown House in Rockcliffe, overlooking the salt flats of the Solway Firth where the River Eden flows into the sea. He was rather an unconventional character who had bought himself out of an unsuccessful army career and, although not Jewish, affected the appearance of an Orthodox Jew and studied Jewish history. He erected the pillar to mark his completion of a walk from his home in Rockcliffe along the length of the river to its source.

It is inscribed with some text in Latin and Greek. The Greek inscription starts "Seek the river of the soul, whence it springs" and equates his journey with the prospect of an anticipated place in heaven. The Latin text conveys the more grounded statement, "William Mounsey, a lone traveller, having commenced his journey at the mouth and finished at the source, fulfilled his vow to the genius and nymphs of the Eden on the 15th March 1850." There is also one of Andy Goldsworthy's Pinfold cairns hidden behind the house at the top end of the village green. Goldsworthy built six of these egg-shaped cairns in six Upper Eden villages as part of his countywide *Sheepfolds* project (see Chapter Ten).

* * *

This summer did I cause a wall of lime and stone to be built round about that piece of ground which I had taken in about Pendragon Castle, of about 10 quarters in height and 90 roodes in compasse, and two gates to be made to lett in horses and coaches. And within the sayd wall I caused to be built a stable and coach house, a brewhouse, bakehouse and wash-house, and a little chamber over the gate that is arched.

From the diary of Lady Anne Clifford, 1662

A little further along the road sits the charismatic eight-hundred-year-old ruin of Pendragon Castle. The name Pendragon is Celtic for 'Commander in Chief'. The supposition that it was occupied by Uther Pendragon and his son, the mythical Celtic hero King Arthur, is unlikely to be true because castles were not built of stone until the much later Norman period. The Norman knight Hugh de Morville was one of its earliest owners, in the twelfth century, when it would have been three storeys high with a ground floor basement, a great hall and vaulted chambers.

The castle was burned down by Scottish raiders on numerous occasions over the years. Later owners included two remark-ably independent women, Lady Idonea de Veteripont in the fourteenth century and the indomitable Lady Anne Clifford in the seventeenth. Both women had acquired the building in a ruinous state and restored it to its former glory, but after Lady Anne died it was dismantled, plundered for its stone and left to the ravages of the weather. Lady Anne had inherited Pendragon when she was sixty years old, along with her three other cas-tles at Brough, Appleby and Brougham. Despite her advancing years, she then devoted the remainder of her life to restoring, improving and living in each of them in turn, for months at a time, as she moved around her Westmorland estates. She was eighty-six when she died.

Prior to Hugh de Morville's time, Celts and Saxons constructed fortresses with wooden stakes, so there is every possibility that a succession of fortified timber structures preceded the stone castle on the site. There are no documentary references to the name Pendragon Castle, however, until the fourteenth century, so perhaps it was Lady Idonea de Veteripoint who named it because she liked the mysterious Arthurian frisson it gave to her isolated and lonely Westmorland residence.

The ruin is now managed by Pendragon Estates, which replaced its recently deceased owner, local landowner and naturalist Juliet Frankland. It was purchased in 1962 for £525 by Juliet's late husband, Raven Frankland, who had the walls consolidated and pointed with lime mortar to prevent further deterioration.

* * *

The future flutters on the wing of a dragonfly
*   as it soars by with our dreams.*
Forever, we hold hands,
the hope and love still shining in our eyes.

Oonagh Monaghan

On the afternoon of July 8, 2006 my daughter Oonagh and her partner Chris, with Juliet's kind permission, held a Humanist wedding here. Secular Humanism has a non-theistic philosophy of life and a framework of convictions providing the basis for a moral outlook without recourse to any notion of the supernatural. Nevertheless, the occasion had much in common with a traditional church wedding, and they exchanged marriage vows and rings and drank sweet violet wine from a 'loving cup' in a ceremony borrowed from the Celts. Nature's glorious landscape was our church on that utopian day. When the ceremony finished, a family of oystercatchers flew overhead, as if on cue, like aerobatic harlequins, piercing the air with a jubilant fanfare of whistling.

Four

Springtime

The next section of Lady Anne's Highway was surfaced with tarmac after the Second World War as part of the Tommy Road, which crosses the fell to join the main road between Sedbergh and Kirkby Stephen. Twisting its way up behind the castle, crossing the River Eden on a bridge first built by Lady Anne, her route veers off to the right onto a rough track again. The river emerges at the bottom of a steeply plummeting slope from behind the preceding hill, with a flourish swollen by the constant recruitment of numerous converging becks.

There is a lime kiln here on the fell to the left, well preserved with its neat arch still intact. Once used to burn limestone quarried in the vicinity, the lime dust it produced was spread on the fields as fertiliser, or made into mortar for building and white-wash for painting walls. A few years ago, the kiln served as one of a series of stage sets for the Brough Players, most of whom were local schoolteachers, who acted out the story of Uther Pendragon and Merlin in a series of linked performances on a walk from Pendragon Castle to Stenkrith Park on the outskirts of Kirkby Stephen. As part of the Kirkby Stephen Walking and Countryside Festival, the performance walk was an annual event for a number of years. The walks attracted perambulating audiences of as many as eighty people. Different plays were performed each year, alternating between Uther Pendragon stories and Viking mythology. I liked the first one best. Written by a writer in residence, with help from pupils at Kirkby Stephen Primary School, it was called *Penning the Dragon*. I had asked them to incorporate a conservation theme, and they invented a story about a dragon's egg, representing "our countryside, our land-scape and our life", rescued from imprisonment at Pendragon Castle and carried on a journey back to its birthplace in a cave at Stenkrith Park. The main character was Merlin who materialised intermittently in voluminous puffs of coloured smoke to pose riddles and offer "the gifts of earth, air, water and fire".

Lost in my recollections of their performance as I wandered along, my ears suddenly picked up the ethereal mewing of two buzzards gliding in slow circles across a clear blue sky. Several weeks had passed since my wintry visit to the source of the Eden, and spring had arrived.

Buzzards are big languorous raptors with a tendency to eat ani-mals that are already dead so, to some extent, they are left alone to their thermal surfing. It may not be long before they are joined by red kites. Over a three-year period, commencing during the summer of 2010, ninety red kites were released by the Forestry Commission from Grizedale Forest in the Lake District. This was the final release in a red kite reintroduction programme that had started in 1998, involving eight locations throughout England and Scotland. Superficially similar to buzzards in their behaviour, red kites are identified by the russet red of their plumage and a distinctively forked tail. Primarily carrion eaters, even more so than buzzards, they were once our most widespread bird of prey, com-monly seen in medieval times scavenging in the rubbish-strewn, rat and mouse infested streets of our cities. By the end of the nine-teenth century, relentless persecution led to their total extinction in England and Scotland and left fewer than a dozen survivors in Wales. With concerted conservation measures in recent years the Welsh red kite population has increased to complement an expanding population of over 2,000 reintroduced birds across the UK. Experts assure us that they coexist with buzzards.

SPRINGTIME

The grassy track continues along the lower contours of Birkett Common leading downhill to a flat expanse of ground closer to the river, where I added a pair of wheatear to my list of newly arriving spring birds. The male was *chack, chacking* as it flew in front of me, displaying its bright white rump. I used to think they were named wheatear because the pattern on the sides of their heads vaguely resembles the shape of an ear of wheat, but the name actually derives from the much less subtle but appropriate description 'white arse'.

Dalefoot Farmhouse, on the other side of the river, is on the site of a house called Blue Grass, which in Lady Anne Clifford's time was the tenanted home of Robert Atkinson, who she refers to in her diary as her "great enemie". My impression when I first read about him in Lady Anne's diaries was that he must have been a bad-tempered hooligan, but I later modified my opinion when I realised he was, in effect, waging his own personal war with the landowning gentry. Lady Anne was *his* great enemy.

This was a time of widespread unrest. The Civil War had ended in chaos and left ordinary people seething with resentment. There was a class war simmering, and grassroots rebellion was rife. Lady Anne, a staunch Royalist, was extremely wealthy, whereas most people in Mallerstang, Ravenstonedale and Kirkby Stephen were poor and thoroughly downtrodden by the rich upper classes. The Quakers were emerging as a significant rebellious force, promoting their cause by peaceful means, but being thrown into prison anyway. Robert Atkinson didn't share their pacifist convictions. He was a volatile character who had killed another resident of Mallerstang in a sword fight near Pendragon Castle and, as a republican captain in Oliver Cromwell's Parliamentary army, fought in the Civil War against King Charles I and was Parliamentary Governor of her Roundhead-occupied castle in Appleby from 1645 to 1648. But it was probably his refusal to pay arrears in rent and manorial tithes in Mallerstang, accrued in her absence, that really annoyed Lady Anne. He was arrested, tried for treason and executed for leading the Kaber Rigg Plot, an abortive uprising in 1663, which included an attempt to recapture Appleby Castle.

An interesting footnote to this trial, to Lady Anne's great credit, is the fact that she befriended Atkinson's widow thereafter, regularly inviting her to dinner and allowing her to remain, with her children, as a tenant of Blue Grass at a much-reduced rent.

As the path veers up the fell, overlooking and parallel with a wide shingle bank in the river, a quite different landscape comes into view. The flatter lie of the land here has been exploited by more intensive farming methods, its human and natural history destroyed by the removal of old field boundaries, the ploughing out of ancient herb-rich turf, reseeding with rye grass and regular application of herbicides and artificial fertiliser. The lush, almost luminous green sward is the backdrop to a dilapidated fourteenth-century pele tower called Lammerside Castle. Not much is known about it, and nobody seems to care that it is close to total collapse.

The bright green fields were crowded with a mix of crossbred ewes and their milk-fat twin lambs languishing nearby; a few swallows, hungry after the exertions of their long flights, twisted and turned in pursuit of the flies buzzing around in clouds just inches above the sleepy ewes' woolly heads. Oystercatchers are numerous on this stretch of the river. I saw four pairs, sitting on the heaps of shingle together, peering down their long red beaks. They certainly don't seem to mind the uniformity of the grass monoculture. I always grin when I see them. They arrive inland in the spring to breed, along with lapwing and curlew, but have a bemused 'morning after the night before' appearance, still resplendent in their black-and-white best bibs and tuckers.

Further on there is an extensive area either side of the river that has been planted with native trees, where I hoped I might see more summer migrants. It would have been gratifying to hear some early chiffchaffs or wood warblers, but all I could hear was the persistent bleating of the sheep. Birdwatching is as much dependent on listening as it is on looking, and there are several birds I can't hear any more, due to slight deafness in my advancing years, particularly those with higher-pitched calls, like goldcrests.

A bird I *can* still hear is the fieldfare. As I rounded a corner into the next field, a large noisy congregation of these handsome Scandinavian thrushes had assembled at the top of a tall sycamore tree, filling the trembling, leaf-layered crown with a crescendo of guttural chattering. Unlike the other migrants I encountered that morning, these birds would soon be leaving Britain for the summer. As I went by a few fluttered out and then hurried back to the safety of their crowded sycamore departure lounge, from where they would fly to some distant Norwegian wood.

Wharton Hall is at the heart of an extensive and busy working modern farm. The older parts are in ruins, but the main house is impressively well preserved, dating from the sixteenth century, when it was the home of Lord Thomas Wharton. The current owners kindly allowed its garden to be used as another stopping place for the performance walks. Whenever I walk along here, my ears still resound to medieval music and the clash of lances and swords wielded by Sir Cumference and Sir Prise, two hopelessly inept knights in cardboard armour, jousting with hilarious pantomime imprecision on the lawn.

The public right of way at Wharton Hall is a designated bridleway, which used to go immediately past the house and through the farmyard, but was officially diverted several years ago, ostensibly to provide a safer route to avoid the tractors and dangerous farm machinery. In fact, more pertinently from my point of view, the diversion was a vital part of a wider-ranging deal I negotiated with the farmer to achieve a new public footpath, across several of his fields, between Kirkby Stephen's isolated railway station and the town. From my earliest years working in countryside management I have often been frustrated with the cumbersome bureaucracy that deters reasonable attempts to rationalise public rights of way.

Networks of footpaths, bridleways and byways are part of our cultural landscape heritage. They facilitate a deeper engagement with the landscape and allow us to inhabit its nooks and crannies more intimately. Most public paths have existed for centuries, and many quite literally enable us to follow in the footsteps of our predecessors, from the earliest of Bronze Age travellers to the twentieth-century postmen who, not so long ago, delivered mail on foot to all the outlying farmhouses. The majority of paths evolved for these utilitarian purposes, and I see no reason why making little adjustments to paths that follow illogical routes can't be made easier, in a recreational context, to avoid farmyards and domestic buildings. A major obstacle is the expense of the legal processes currently considered necessary. Any application for change has to be advertised in the local newspaper, and there are solicitor's costs, which escalate if there are objections from any member of the public, thus necessitating a public enquiry.

Crucially, the impact on the public's enjoyment has to be carefully considered when diverting a path. The owner of Wharton Hall had expressed his concern about the risks of injury to those using the bridleway through his farmyard, and we discussed the relative merits of a diversion. There were clear public benefits to be gained, and I offered to consult with potential objectors.

I had long been aware that a safe footpath was needed between Kirkby Stephen railway station and the town to avoid the main road. Here was an opportunity to secure a minor path diversion on one part of a farm that would significantly improve public safety and enjoyment, with the additional offer of a major, wholly new path on another.

Unfortunately, Railtrack resisted the proposal at the station, despite the fact that people arriving by train would benefit from a safe alternative footpath. Long-winded negotiations delayed dedication of the new public footpath for a full five years. Ten years later the County Council found funding to purchase the strip of land occupied by the path, upgraded its classification to cycleway, fenced it off and resurfaced it. At long last.

Five

Stenkrith Park

I turned onto a footpath leading to the river. The speed of the river quickens here as it changes direction through a narrow ravine, funnelling its way below the arch of the road bridge and swirling between and over huge slabs of potholed, water-worn stone.

I crossed the road into Stenkrith Park, where the new foliage on an understory of twisted hawthorn trees was catching the sunlight and glowing like an effervescent green mist. Stenkrith Park is one of those special places that exudes an ambience all of its own. A genius loci surely resides here, if not a community of fairies. I inhaled the pungent smell of wild garlic and descended the well-trodden track to walk with the river again. The garlic wasn't yet in flower, but the ground was bright with the starry white petals of wood anemones, a few yellow patches of prim-roses, daffodils and celandines and tiny clusters of purple violets. The river emerges from below the neat stone arch of the road bridge and the elegant curve of the blue metal footbridge, veiled by the lace of overhanging trees.

The galvanised steel footbridge strikes a Victorian note in style, but is only recent, having been built to coincide with the Millennium. Its installation was delayed until 2002 because of the access restrictions imposed during the foot and mouth epidemic the previous year. Designed by Charles Blackett-Ord, a local civil engineer, it was commissioned to provide a pedestrian crossing to connect with the redundant railway track, which now provides recreational access between Stenkrith and Hartley. It is the brainchild of Mike Sunderland, a local schoolteacher who was incensed when a dilapidated fence across the track at the Hartley end was renewed to prevent public access. He decided to investigate its ownership and discovered, to his surprise, that most of it was still owned by Railtrack.

As the line includes two picturesque viaducts, Podgill and Merrygill, he contacted the Northern Viaduct Trust, an organisation set up to renovate obsolete railway viaducts. In due course, the Trust purchased the line, found the money to restore it and converted it into a new route for walkers, cyclists, horseriders and wheelchair users. Mike drove the plans forward and his project management skills ensured that the highest quality was achieved in every detail.

The footbridge provides a viewing platform from which to look down at the cascading water in the gorge almost 13 metres below. A great elliptical-shaped crater has been scooped out of the rock by the river's powerful current and the abrasive, churning scree of small stones it carries. This has been known as the Devil's Mustard Mill and, more logically, the Coopkarnel, a Danish word meaning 'cup-shaped chasm'.

Stenkrith is like a tiny vestigial forest, much of it coppiced in the past. The landscape we have around Kirkby Stephen today, with its patchwork of fields, dry-stone walls, hedges, small woods and shelter belts along the river valley and rising up to the high bare hills, is the result of an uneasy alliance between farmers and nature that started thousands of years ago. Nowadays it is predominately sheep-rearing country, and farmers are no longer so concordant with nature. Some cattle are kept, but the hill farmers' year mainly revolves around the care of sheep, with a particular focus on the Swaledale breed.

In prehistoric times this was a wooded wilderness, teeming with wildlife, where our earliest ancestors, hunter-gatherers, made small clearings for their huts. As time went on and agricultural skills developed, trees were cleared to make way for crops and grazing animals. By the thirteenth century almost nothing of the original wildwood survived and most of the remaining fragments were managed for timber production. In the succeeding centuries, as marshy valleys were drained and agriculture evolved to become more centralised and efficient, some of the cleared woodland on marginal land regenerated, and farming practice, based on a system of commoners' rights, coexisted in harmony with nature. Small woods were coppiced in rotation, maintaining many of the larger wildwoods' ecological characteristics where flowers, insects and birds thrived.

I've always been interested in coppicing; I used to spend time doing this when I worked on National Nature Reserves in Somerset and Wiltshire. My primary aim then was nature conservation. Coppiced woodland greatly benefits wildlife, speeding up the natural processes of the once-extensive ancient wildwood of Mesolithic and Palaeolithic times. As moribund trees fell, little clearings appeared, letting in more light so that a diverse range of flora and fauna could thrive. Coppicing mimics this over a much shorter time scale. Like herb-rich meadow management, coppiced woodland is another example of human intervention in harmony with nature. It takes advantage of the self-renewing ability of deciduous trees such as hazel, ash, birch and oak, which grow new shoots from the stumps after they have been cut down. These continue to grow and, if cut at intervals of ten to twenty years in a succession of compartments throughout a wood, will go on producing long stems indefinitely.

The original purpose of coppicing was to harvest for use in a range of products, with each species of tree offering particular properties. Hazel was used to make hurdles, birch for bobbins as spools for cotton thread, ash for tool handles, and alder for charcoal burning. I once spent a long day with a hurdle maker trying to split whole lengths of hazel poles with a billhook. After several hours I had to admit defeat, with hundreds of short bits in a heap up to my knees. Ancient woodland crafts demand considerable skill, and thankfully many have been revived in recent years in conjunction with nature conservation.

Since the Second World War huge advances in agricultural productivity and transport have made it possible for farmers to override ecological processes. Developments in mechanisation and chemical technology subject wildlife to extreme pressures. Nature conservation is now dependent on modern farmers making a conscious effort to include habitat management as an integral part of their work. Farmers today don't have an easy job trying to combine wildlife habitat management with food production.

Kirkby Stephen's landscape is spectacularly lovely. Local farmers are quick to agree that this makes it a very special area in which to live and work. Some seem less prepared to admit that an ecologically robust countryside is a crucial factor in maintaining the high quality of their meat and dairy products, along with acknowledging the importance of recreational access and tourism in support of a sustainable rural economy. All these aspects of countryside management are interdependent – and reliant on the ability and willingness of farmers to reconcile conflicting demands on the landscape we all share.

Passage, the second Eden Benchmark sculpture, is located in Stenkrith and is well named. Of all the Benchmarks this is the least popular, partly, I suspect, because it mimics the water-eroded rocks in the river, and people judge it, erroneously in my opinion, as bland and unimaginative. Laura White, the artist concerned, was anxious to avoid making a sculpture that would impose discordantly on what she recognised is a sensitive site.

She had just returned from a sculpture symposium in Japan when she started her residency in Kirkby Stephen and had been inspired by the 'less is more' philosophy of Japanese culture. The shapes she carved in the stones are clearly derived from the shapes she observed in the riverbed boulders but carefully refined, as if words in a poem. Just as the sculpture incorporates a space through its middle, representing the confined passage of the river under the bridge beyond, so its function as an unobtrusive place to sit is assimilated by our enjoyment of Stenkrith Park. Unfortunately, Laura's choice of stone proved to be a mistake. Instead of a hard Cumbrian limestone she chose Ancaster Limestone, a softer stone quarried in Lincolnshire with a characteristic blue veining, which conveys an impression of flowing water. I liked the idea too, at the time, but what we hadn't anticipated was its propensity to crumble. Its critics will be pleased.

I sat for a while, contented, immersed in the green light of this arboreal sanctuary, listening to the music of the water and relishing the wise counsel and visual theatre of the trees. Sheltered on the far side below a high, steep, tree-covered bank, this stretch of the river is endlessly fascinating, stretching wide as it percolates through serried ranks of fissured and perforated blocks of flat rock. On days of heavy rain, the blocks disappear under a rampage of swirling whirlpools filled with pebbles, which resume their frenetic grinding of the *coop*-shaped holes. On calmer summer days the river subsides and children collect the polished pebbles in buckets, spending happy hours playing, paddling and picnicking, just as they would at the seaside.

Geologically, Stenkrith is the place where the pale grey limestone of the Dales meets the dark red sandstone of the Eden Valley, and most of the rock is a naturally occurring conglomerate of the two, called Brockram, consisting of limestone fragments cemented in highly compressed sandstone.

STENKRITH PARK

Two dippers were flying back and forth, alighting on the stones, bobbing and curtseying to each other in an elegant waltz and, every so often, plunging underwater in search of insect sustenance. Chocolate brown with expansive white chests and twitching tails, they sing a sweet, rippling song. They were suddenly joined by a pair of grey wagtails stealing the limelight, dashing from boulder to boulder with long slender tails bouncing in time to the tempo of the rushing water.

Six

The Poetry Path

Coltsfoot, celandine, earliest daisies.
Twin lambs race to the mother, baby cries...

From 'April Poem', by Meg Peacocke

Stenkrith Park is on the route of the Poetry Path, a series of twelve poems carved on large stones, each written on the theme of a year in the life of a hill farmer. Encouraged by the success of Eden Benchmarks, I had wanted to do something similar in the wake of 2001, the dreadful year when life in Cumbria was paralysed by foot and mouth disease and many farmers were forced to destroy all their livestock. As they started to recover and buy in new stock, it seemed an appropriate time to acknowledge the hill farmer's historic relationship with the landscape in and around the upper Eden Valley.

The route starts on the outskirts of Kirkby Stephen, along the Nateby road, at the bottom of a grassy track called Bollam Lane, where it meets the River Eden. It crosses the river on a wooden footbridge known as Swingy Bridge and turns south along a deeply worn, hedge-lined bridleway to the Podgill Railway Path. It then goes west to Stenkrith, back over the river again on the Millennium Footbridge and returns north from there, back to Swingy Bridge. The twelve poems, one for each month of the year, were written by the distinguished poet Meg Peacocke and carved by hand by stone lettering artist Pip Hall. The stones sit at intervals along the route and feature Pip's decorative motifs depicting some of the activities associated with every month of the hill farmer's year. Rubbings can be taken from these on sheets of paper with crayons.

I like the permanence of stone. The Eden Valley hosts numerous man-made stone structures in the landscape that have survived from antiquity, communicating our ancestor's reflections on life and eternity across the centuries. Who is to say that archaic stone circles like Long Meg and Her Daughters near Little Salkeld were not the work of a Neolithic artist? Whatever their original purpose, they somehow still articulate to this day the imperative of humankind's oneness with our Mother Earth. Never before has this insight been more compelling, yet so ignored, as it is today.

My aim with the Poetry Path was to introduce a contemporary equivalent for the twenty-first century, which itself becomes an integrated part of the heritage it promotes. Locals helped me select a poet and a letter carver from a shortlist I'd compiled of likely candidates. From a strong field, both Meg and Pip were our unanimous choice.

Management of the Eden Benchmarks project had convinced me that a paramount constituent of the public art commissioning process was to keep the artist's brief as non-prescriptive as possible. I resisted the frequently expressed expectation that each artist should be required to secure approval of their intentions with a representational drawing or maquette before making their sculpture. Apart from the impossibility of gaining an entire community's agreement, or even the accord of a representative committee, it is my view that if we want art in the landscape, we must allow the artists as much freedom of expression as possible. Emile Zola described a work of art as being the product of an artist looking at the world "through a temperament". It is the artists' function after all, albeit within the parameters of site specificity, to understand and creatively communicate their own feelings about a place.

After I took the first tentative steps toward implementing the Poetry Path, it became obvious that the initial outline of what I'd had in mind fell well short of the project's full potential. My vision was based on little more than instinctive optimism and an ardent conviction that poems carved in stone would be an interesting way to achieve my aims as a 'countryside interpreter'. From the moment I introduced Meg and Pip to one another they quickly established a rapport, took ownership of the framework of the proposal and, in the ensuing months, transformed it with something akin to alchemy.

Pip Hall teaches letter carving courses and workshops in Cumbria and elsewhere. I particularly like the way she experiments with the forms of letters, orchestrating their relationship with each other to reflect the rhythm and meaning of text. It had been obvious from her job application that she loves and appreciates poetry, and I wasn't surprised to discover that she is also an accomplished musician. There is surely a correlation between music, poetry and the flow and flair of good calligraphy, and Pip has an intuitive aptitude for all three in abundance.

Meg Peacocke ran a smallholding on Stainmore for many years, so she knew all about a farmer's life. She has published five critically acclaimed collections of poems and is a winner of the prestigious Cholmondeley Award for distinction in poetry. I'd never met her before, although I was already familiar with some of her poems as I had a copy of her first published collection, *Marginal Land,* on my bookshelf. I found some of the poems difficult, but good poetry can't be read like prose. Like a fine malt whisky, a poem is distilled and concentrated, honed to perfection and reduced to the essence of its meaning. Working with Meg I slowly gleaned insight into the importance of structure in a poem: the shape, pattern and movement that runs through it and gives it life, the implication of meaning rather than elemental description, the length of its lines and their arrangement in stanzas, the length and stress of syllables in relation to one another, and their beat, rhythm and metre. These are the tricks of the poet's trade – but the best poets keep them hidden with a conjurer's sleight of hand.

When Meg was offered the job, she had some reservations. She had always written for herself rather than to commission and she knew she would have to write poems that would be more instantly accessible than those she normally writes, which sit on a page to be savoured and unravelled slowly. She also had misgivings about the intrusiveness of public art, compounded by the prospect of seeing poems she had written herself displayed permanently along the route of one of her favourite walks. Fortunately, she overcame her doubts and in due course delivered the poems. Her brief had been that the poetry should document each month of the farmers' year, so I was disconcerted when only four of the twelve poems were specifically about farming. I was nervous when we met to discuss this, because Meg is always forthright, but in no time at all she quietly allayed my fears. She explained that the poems were intended to evoke the wider context of the farmer's life. They are, of course, about the farmers' year: the animals, the weather, soil and the geological lie of the land, wild water and nature, human history and the river that cuts a timeless swathe through the lives of all of us who live in East Cumbria. I was instantly convinced.

I first met Pip when I attended her letter-carving course in Martindale, near Ullswater, shortly before she was due to start work on the Poetry Path. This gave us an opportunity to discuss the project. I'd envisaged a trail consisting of twelve poems carved in different lettering styles on long, thin slabs of stone, incorporated into stone wall stiles. I wanted to call this 'Twelve Poems in Twelve Different Stiles'. I spent months searching the length and breadth of Upper Eden for a suitably sequenced series of twelve stiles in a circular route that would fit with the title. It was only my failure to find one that made me realise I was over-looking the ideal route, between Kirkby Stephen and Stenkrith Park, right on my doorstep, for the sake of what had become an obsessive preoccupation with a pun!

I still had in mind using the long, thin slabs of stone, not least because they could easily be transported to a letter carver's studio and then brought back and set into the ground along the route as standing stones. I hadn't budgeted to provide either accom-modation or a workshop for the artist, so when it transpired that Pip had a friend living near Kendal who could accommodate the artists free of charge, it wasn't long before I found myself wandering around a local quarry with Pip and Meg, looking at a variety of large, irregularly shaped rocks. My notion of the neat procession of long, thin slabs of stone was laid to rest.

Meg wrote her poems with the specific locations in mind, and we chose the stones accordingly. We also decided to use a mix of limestone and red sandstone to reflect the geology at Stenkrith. I organised a haulage contractor to move the first of these to Pip's workshop, and we found a second-hand gantry so that Pip could move the stones around within the workshop. Without further ado, she then embarked on the gargantuan task of chiselling each of the 1,752 letters of Meg's twelve poems by hand, with exqui-site precision, on nineteen hard blocks of stone, millions of years old. She designed twelve lettering styles and a distinct layout for each poem to enhance their visual impact and carved the small motifs representing key activities of the hill farmers' year. When each stone was completed and transported to site ready for installation, all three of us deliberated together on their exact placement and positioning.

January's poetry stone is the winter stone, "wind a blade, trees stripped", and nestles unobtrusively in the tree-latticed tunnel of Bollam Lane, just before the point where a bridleway, hoof-hollowed by centuries of horse traffic, fords the River Eden.

Across the river the February poem describes the ache for winter's end. It is inscribed on a stack of four limestone blocks, mimicking the cornerstones of a nearby ruined byre, where wintering cattle once sheltered, "safe from reiving wind and rain".

Bearing right onto a hedge-lined path, once the main thoroughfare between Kirkby Stephen and Mallerstang, the track slopes down into a shallow gill where the red sandstone pillar bearing the March poem stands in a beck.

> *"From field*
>   *and fell*
> *run cold*
>   *run small......"*

This was an exciting one to install. The contractor used a low loader with a telescopic arm. For the other sites, each stone was slung on heavy duty straps to be lowered into place, and any adjustment was easily achieved whilst the stone was still suspended just above the ground. This stone, however, was to be installed in a pool of water where the beck tumbles off a vertical shelf of red sandstone, above which there is a potentially unstable grassy slope at the top of the bank opposite. Because of the narrowness of the path the contractor had no alternative but to approach the beck from the other side and chain the low loader to a tractor to avoid it falling over the edge. The poetry stone was then suspended on straps from the end of the telescopic arm and cautiously propelled forward. It swung gently above the pool. Meg, Pip and I had been joined by a group of friendly walkers, and a lively discussion ensued as to how we might position the stone in the beck to its best advantage. We were all inclined to favour a central position, but not at all certain if it would sit securely enough in the stony morass at the bottom of the pool. I had tried wading into the water to dig a hole, without much success. As we hesitated, mesmerised by the dangling stone, one of the straps snapped, and it plunged with a mighty splash into the beck. There is wedged itself firmly in an upright position against the sandstone outcrop at the back of the pool. It was as if the poem had lost patience with our prevarication. We all roared our delight at this unexpected and most satisfactory of outcomes. It was one of those lucky accidents that defied logic. As I turned to look at Meg and Pip, I could have sworn they exchanged conspiratorial smiles.

The path continues uphill, along another sunken hollow way, enveloped by a canopy of trees. Halfway up the slope, April's poem is on a stone that has been incorporated into a section of dry-stone wall, celebrating lambing time and the new lambs huddling behind their mothers, "braced against these April suns and sleets."

The poem for May, also built into a wall, is on a big slab of red sandstone, its ripe peach colour contrasting dramatically with the grey blocks of limestone in the wall around it and incised with a curly lettering style reminiscent of wool. This poem is about the shepherd, "seamed with muck and the sweat runs into his eyes," removing dirty clumps of fleece from the tails of his rams.

The path crosses a bridge above the railway path to where the June poem is situated. Carved on an industrial block of gritstone, it describes the beauty of elder blossom in the spring sunshine "while fledglings try small quivery leaps".

The route then follows a section of the Railway Path, where there are three poetry stones. July's poem is a succinctly lyrical equation encapsulating the imperative of making hay (and silage) while the sun shines. Pip's calligraphic invention mimics not only the "the first green furrow" and the "ark of weather" in the poem but also, as a farmer's small son pointed out to me one day, the tread marks of a tractor tyre.

The August stone sits amongst the trees and is perhaps the one I like best. It is inscribed on a large piece of red sandstone shaped like a slice of melon, with the curving lines of two stanzas carved on both sides, echoing the semicircular shape of the stone. The lettering is jauntily curvy as well and big and bold, like the script on a Salvation Army banner.

For touch, taste, smell, sight, hearing
I give thanks.

In August farmers show off their sheep at agricultural shows and hope to win prizes for their best animals. When I was last there, Pip's motif of a prize-winning Swaledale tup's head had been enlivened with a colourful wreath of scribbled marks left behind by a child who'd taken a rubbing from it with a crayon.

The disused railway the path follows was constructed between 1857 and 1860 to facilitate steam locomotives pulling coal from the Durham coalfields to the shipyards at Barrow-in-Furness. It closed in 1962, and the poem for September, on an oblong block of St Bee's sandstone, urges us to use our imaginations to "Listen, and catch the hiss of steam again."

The railway path terminates at this point, but the Poetry Path continues across the river, back into Stenkrith Park, over the footbridge. Stenkrith Park's intersecting geology is the subject of October's poem, on a recumbent pair of stones where one verse, carved in sandstone, asks the question, "How did we trace a path through the ancient dunes?" The other, on limestone, invites us to ponder, "How did we swim through the drift and not perish?"

The eleventh pair of poetry stones, standing together at the other end of Stenkrith Park, hint at the darker days of November with a tiny carved motif of a farmer preparing his rams for tupping. Two flowing lines of neatly chiselled letters on sleek, flat, polished surfaces celebrate the bigger picture of the river moving "softly or in spate" on its perpetual journey "from Mallerstang to the shifting Solway sands."

The footpath returns across two fields to Bollam Lane, parallel with the river. I can almost always guarantee the sight of a grey heron along here standing motionless on long legs in the shallow water, watching and waiting, ready to lunge at an unsuspecting fish. The heron usually hears me first and takes fright. I enjoy the heron's slow, lanky, pterodactyl manoeuvres, up and away, between tree branches and into the sky. Appropriately for this location, the December poem is a Japanese style haiku about a heron, which concludes the Poetry Path on a pensive, philosophical note with its seventeen syllables. They are carved in three short lines on a row of three narrow horizontal stones.

Seven

Nine Standards

The weird sisters, hand in hand,
Posters of the sea and land,
Thus do go about, about:
THRICE TO THINE AND THRICE TO MINE
AND THRICE AGAIN, TO MAKE UP NINE.

From *Macbeth*, by William Shakespeare

Swingy Bridge doesn't swing anymore – although presumably it did in the 1960s. The river has a history of rock 'n' roll
excess here, bombarding and destabilising the bridge with trees
uprooted in fits of rain-fuelled fury further upstream. The structure of the bridge has been replaced and strengthened over many
years. It had new beams fitted during my time with ECCP, which
bent into a bow shape a year later after a tree trunk hit the middle
pier and pushed it out of line. The bridge remained stable, but
whenever I crossed it, I half expected the pier might suddenly
snap back into its central position and shoot me through the air.
A new abutment has been constructed since then and the middle
pier replaced with a more secure foundation on the riverbed.

I stood as I've done hundreds of times watching the river
upstream and down, hoping to see an otter. The water was a
golden brown, a rich blend of enfolded sunshine and dissolving
peat from the hills, but there was no circle made bright by the
sudden appearance of an otter's head. Experienced naturalists tell
me that I would have a much better chance of seeing one if I

came out very early in the morning. Fishermen tell me they see otters in the River Eden at all times of the day.

Parting company with the river on the other side of the bridge, I followed the path between the stacked stone blocks of the February poem and the derelict byre. I turned left towards Kirkby Stephen along the narrow hedged lonning that was once a busy packhorse trail between Kirkby Stephen and Nateby. The lonning gives way to an outlying remnant of deciduous woodland consisting mainly of beech, oak, elm and sycamore standing like gentle giants with their heads reaching for the sky. My appreciation of nature has always been emotionally and aesthetically driven. The scientific dimension mostly eludes me, to a large extent due to what Samuel Taylor Coleridge's wayward son Hartley called "the woeful impotence of weak resolve". Rather belatedly, as I've got older, some elementary science has crept into my wishy-washy perception of the world. I still take pleasure in trees as living sculptures, but I am much more aware of their biology and the power-house energy of their life cycle and wider ecological significance.

A red squirrel scampered in front of me, instantly lightening my despondent mood. Eden is still a stronghold for red squirrels, although grey squirrels are increasingly evident, spreading up from other parts of England where red squirrels are extinct, and threatening to extinguish the red population in this area as well. Grey squirrels eat most of the available food and carry a pox virus that is harmless to them but fatal to their indigenous red counterpart.

Tragically, within my lifetime it has become almost impossible to enjoy wildlife without worrying about doom-laden issues relating to species decline, but I can still savour glorious moments like these, shining like beacons through the gloom. This one was like a sunburst of defiance. Chestnut red and bright-eyed, the squirrel paused to glance at me, flouncing its flaming orange tail before hopping into the undergrowth, only to emerge a few seconds later halfway up a beech tree. There, it settled on a branch for a prolonged preening session. I watched until my neck ached and I was forced to move, despite which the squirrel continued to preen and completely ignore me as I walked on down the track to the footbridge over Ladthwaite Beck and into the adjoining field.

Ladthwaite Beck twists its way out of the wood here, swerving below a sequestered vertical face of red sandstone before slipping into the River Eden, which reappears obligingly at this point, as if to keep me company again as I walk along the lower edge of the field.

The beck comes down from Hartley Fell and is propelled through a sloping woodland called Ewbank Scar Wood, along a narrow chute of glistening rock at the base of a precipitous white, carboniferous limestone cliff. The woodland is an officially designated Site of Special Scientific Interest. Its importance relates to species-rich limestone grassland and ancient semi-natural woodland that has survived over many hundreds of years. It supports five nationally uncommon plant species and a breeding population of the rare Northern Brown Argus butterfly. I opened up a public footpath that had been lost for many years in an impenetrable tangle of trees, as part of the Discover Eden Project, which improved and waymarked fourteen circular walking routes on public paths at locations throughout East Cumbria, to showcase the scenic diversity of the Eden catchment landscape.

The area around Kirkby Stephen is well endowed with footpaths and bridleways, but I was unable to resist a route up to the nine stone cairns known as the Nine Standards, which stand in a line like sentinels on the distant horizon of Hartley Fell. The path through Ewbank Scar Wood provided a scenically gratifying link up to the fell from the town. I'd had difficulty on previous visits identifying the path accurately in a bewildering maze of contouring ridges criss-crossing the steeply sloping wood, all of them obstructed by sprawling and fallen trees. Surveying a path in those conditions by eye, with only a small-scale map as a guide, is always a challenge, but I also suspected the line of the path must have been one that was hastily scrawled on the original 1950s draft of the 'Definitive' Public Path map by a parish councillor who hadn't had time to check it on the ground. After several exploratory visits I chose a line of least resistance, making sure it descended along some of its length in close proximity to Ladthwaite Beck, to provide some good views of the limestone cliff before rising again to the top edge of the wood. Some years later, a landslip completely obliterated the path.

The Eden flows on a straight course as it approaches Kirkby Stephen, still very much in its infancy, only 16 kilometres from its source above Mallerstang. This is an idyllic spot, lined generously with alder trees, where I sometimes see kingfishers and often linger for a while searching for pebbles that have a spherical or elliptical symmetry. I like their smooth, water-hewn perfection, which encapsulates the progress of the river over lapsed centuries with utter simplicity. I have an expanding collection, resembling a clutch of fossilised dinosaurs' eggs, in a corner of my garden.

Hartley Castle Farmhouse, up across the fields to the right, stands on a site where there was once a castle. It was originally the home of Sir Andrew (or Andreas) de Harcla, Sheriff of Cumberland, who led many battles against the Scots, culminating in the English defeat at Bannockburn in 1314. He was executed for treason by King Edward III following some questionable, although almost certainly well-meaning negotiations with Robert the Bruce in 1325. His estate was subsequently sold to the Musgrave family. The castle was described in 1677 as "an Elizabethan building consisting of an inner quadrangle, surrounded by buildings and an outer courtyard to the north protected by a high and thick curtain wall. The south end was occupied by the chapel and withdrawing rooms, whilst on the western side, a large oriel window lit a long gallery facing the quadrangle." The Musgrave family lived there until 1735 when it was demolished. There is no public access to the farmhouse.

The path up to Kirkby Stephen crosses the Eden over a stone bridge known as Franks Bridge, built at about the same time using some of the stone from the castle. The views from the bridge compel me to stop and stare. The river itself is reason enough, but on a clear day there is also an excellent view of the Nine Standards cairns on top of Hartley Fell. Nobody knows why they were built, but there have been some audacious claims regarding their age and function. In their present form, give or take some restoration work over the years, I don't think they can be more than two hundred years old. There is some evidence to suggest that nine stone markers existed previously, but they were regularly called stones rather than cairns. Certainly, the name Nine Standards is mentioned in centuries-old boundary inspection documents and the area around the summit was known as Nine Standards Rigg and shown on maps dating from more than four hundred years ago. There haven't been any specific descriptions, or even indications, of nine markers in a straight row as they are today. Could it be that the original Nine Standards were standing stones rather than cairns and perhaps differently aligned? They are often confused with Nine Stones Rig in the Scottish Borders made famous as "Nine Stane Hill", in Walter Scott's poem *Bridal of Triermain*.

THE STREAM INVITES US TO FOLLOW

And redden'd all the Nine-stane Hill
And the shrieks of death, that wildly broke
Through devouring flame and smothering smoke,
Made the warrior's heart blood chill!

Up close, our present-day Nine Standards have a reassuring quality, like a row of amiable trolls transfixed on the skyline. If only they could speak. I usually talk to them when I'm up there, if nobody else is around, but they remain resolutely silent. Varied in shape and size, the middle one is the biggest and most impressive. Essentially cone-shaped, it is 3.5 metres tall and 3.7 metres in diameter at its base, tapering to the top with two intermediate ledges around its circumference. Standing in an irregular line, roughly north to south and 75 metres from end to end, all of them are variously cone-shaped except the one at the northern end, which was reconstructed years ago as a square marker column by the Ordnance Survey. Their location, only 12 metres lower but 400 metres south of the summit, was obviously chosen to ensure they could be seen from a wide spectrum of vantage points in the valley below. Had they been built further back on the actual summit, they would have been much less visible.

I instigated some major repairs in 2005 as part of the Discover Eden Project. Most of the cairns were in a severe state of disrepair; two had completely fallen down and the middle one was in a perilously dangerous condition close to collapse. I'd allocated £10,000 from the Heritage Lottery grant for their repair, little suspecting, once again, that my good intentions would be met with more of that all-too-prevalent petty bureaucratic intransigence.

I was aware that the cairns were a designated Listed Building. What I hadn't realised was that their listing didn't necessarily equate to their protection and I was left wondering why legally protected structures can be allowed to deteriorate so badly to a point where they are falling down. I found myself wondering whether listing is simply an official acknowledgement that a building is leaning over to one side!

I'd been in discussion with the County Archaeologist and he had, somewhat unenthusiastically I thought at the time, approved my proposal to repair them on condition that I commissioned an archaeologist to carry out a desk-based documentary survey of their history. I engaged archaeologists at Oxford Archaeology North to do this. In due course they delivered their findings, which convinced me that the cairns we see today are indeed Victorian in origin.

Although the name 'standards' is generally considered to derive from the cairns' similarity to 'standers', the columns of stone left to support the ceilings of tunnels in coal mines, the word has also been used in relation to behaviour. The first headmaster at Kirkby Stephen Primary School, Frank Parrott, exploited the connection (and, I suspect, the close proximity of the cairns to heaven in the eyes of small children) by devising nine standards of good conduct. It wasn't a new idea. The Bible talks about the Fruit of the Holy Spirit being essential attributes of a true Christian life, and there are nine of those too. Kirkby Stephen has a long history of Puritanism and temperance, so a row of stone cairns overlooking the town might have been a Calvinistic alternative to a cross. St Ninian, an early Christian evangelist, travelled throughout the Scottish Lowlands and northern England during the fourth century preaching the same message, and there are several places associated with his visits where his name has, over the centuries, transmuted to the number nine.

So, the intriguing and overriding question is: why are there nine? At one time, nine of the villages and parishes around Kirkby Stephen were referred to as its townships. I wondered if that might have been the reason, until further thought and enquiry unleashed an astonishing line-up of 'nines', many of which invest the number nine with an array of real, religious, mythical or occultist significance.

Beethoven wrote nine symphonies. The French word for nine is *neuf*, which also means new, and the human gestation period from conception to birth is nine months. Noon, our word for midday, means nine and goes back to the Romans' ninth hour after sunrise. The spells cast by witches often included the number nine; their cats had nine lives. There are numerous ancient games with nine components, like shove ha'penny, nine-pin bowling and skittles. The Greeks believed in nine Muses, goddesses who inspired artists, poets, musicians and dancers. Dante's four-teenth-century epic poem *The Divine Comedy* tells of his journey through the nine circles of hell, reflecting the fact that most of the world's religions include stories involving the number nine.

And this leads me back to the Vikings. There were nine worlds in Norse mythology contained within a gigantic tree they called Yggdrasil that also included a frosty realm of ice, lands of giants and elves and the Middle Earth of mortal Vikings themselves. As the Kirkby Stephen area is rooted in Viking culture, could there be a Viking connection? Did the original nine markers represent their nine worlds? And did they once form the shape of a Viking longship? Dead Viking warriors were often cremated, their corpses burned on a funeral pyre set within an enclosure of standing stones arranged to resemble a boat.

Once I had received the results of the documentary survey from Oxford Archaeology North, I submitted an application to Eden District Council for Listed Building Consent to repair or restore the cairns where necessary. The documentary search had unearthed a sequence of photographs, the first of which dated back to 1918 and showed very clearly their height and profile at that time. Later photographs indicated they had been subject to regular repair and their shapes kept more or less the same ever since. I thought it went without saying that their restoration would involve dismantling and rebuilding, as is the case with any dry-stone structure. Witness the hundreds of kilometres of dry-stone walls, many probably older than the Nine Standards, painstakingly kept in good repair by the farmers. Crucially the photographs of the more complex structure of the cairns provided a vital guide to restoring them, as near as possible, to the shape they were in 1918.

So far, so good; I'd felt rather pleased with myself for having secured the funding to reinstate an outstanding and much-loved landmark, which contributes a real sense of place and identity for local residents, regardless of its apparently uncertain historical importance. In my naivety I thought the planning authority would agree, until I received a letter refusing consent to repair them on the basis that a listed building must not be demolished or altered by rebuilding once it has collapsed. According to the planners there was insufficient "overriding exceptional justification" to restore them.

I was shocked. These are dry-stone cairns that have been maintained for at least two hundred years by repeated and skilled rebuilding, when necessary, without alteration. Modern bureaucracy was the reason the Nine Standards had been left to deteriorate for so long – ever since they were designated as a listed structure.

I conveyed my astonishment and bitter disappointment in no uncertain terms to the planning officer. The official letter of refusal offered no room for manoeuvre or compromise. It compared my proposal with a hypothetical plan "to rebuild Stonehenge" and therefore was "not in the best interests of its historic value to society." (In fact, several of the Stonehenge stones were re-erected and set on concrete bases in 1901, 1958 and 1963). The letter did concede that one of the cairns appeared to be dangerously unstable, and therefore this could be "addressed by sensitive repair". Otherwise, however, they should be left "uncompromised". The planners seemed to be missing the whole point. With this authoritarian command, they were condemning the cairns to ruin.

To my relief, the planner I spoke to offered an inkling of hope with an "economical" interpretation of his guarded exposition of the restrictions. I proceeded on the basis that we could repair the cairns (just enough) to make them safe and build a 'new' one in close proximity to the one that had fallen down, which we weren't allowed to rebuild. A few days later Steve Allen, Cumbria's premier dry-stone wall builder, with his two assistants and meticulous reference to the photographs, started work. Within eight days (or was it nine?) the five cairns that had been in a ruinous state looked as good as new, and the remaining four had been 'invisibly' mended. Their work won the North Pennines AONB Conservation Award 2005, and any further comment from the local district authority was conspicuous by its absence.

During the course of the Nine Standards saga, Stephen Walker contacted me to find out more about my restoration efforts. He went on to explain that he had been born and bred in Kirkby Stephen and always believed the cairns were much older than was generally thought. His credentials were impressive. He had worked for an overseas equivalent of the Ordnance Survey, so knew a thing or two about maps and land surveying, and his questions were pertinent. He expressed his disquiet that no proper archaeological or topographical site survey had been implemented prior to the restoration work. He was right; it was a missed opportunity, but really not my responsibility, particularly when I'd been obliged to adopt such clandestine, even underhand tactics simply in order to ensure that our Nine Standards didn't disappear from the skyline forever.

Such is Stephen's conviction that they are extremely old and might even date from the Bronze Age that he wrote a book, *The Nine Standards: Ancient Cairns or Modern Folly?*, largely growing out of his research on the tradition of inspecting manorial boundaries in the Kirkby Stephen area. These were the territory-defining 'perambulations', or 'beating the bounds', regularly undertaken by landowners and local community representatives who walked the boundaries, identifying them by recording prominent features like rivers and streams, ditches and dykes, ridges, hilltops, large boulders, crosses and cairns. Some of these surveys mention the Nine Standards and some do not. His certainty and meticulous research have given me much food for thought.

The same weak resolve that in my early years hindered my acquisition of scientific knowledge has also inhibited my chronological grasp of human history. Stephen may well be right, but I still think the cairns we have today are comparatively recent, built to replace some previous markers and to fulfil our expectations of a hill called Nine Standards Rigg. What I don't accept, though, is his assertion that their survival was assured in earlier times by a tradition that compelled passers-by to add a stone to each cairn. This is true of many smaller cairns that have been built casually by walkers in hill country as route markers, but those are waist high at the most, whereas the tops of the Nine Standards beyond the reach of even the tallest walker, and their construction has obviously been the work of experts. If funding can be scraped together in the future for regular maintenance, by people who know what they are doing, then a stitch in time will save…

Eight

Kirkby Stephen

There are three narrow walled routes up to the town from Frank's Bridge. The widest of these is called Stoneshot and is just about wide enough for the careful passage of a small car. Possibly it was designed to help barricade against attack during the centuries of conflict between England and Scotland. It may have acquired the name from the time when Kirkby Stephen folk defended their town by shooting stones from slings and catapults down the lane and onto the heads of their Scottish invaders.

I like the sensation of emerging from a confined space into an open one and I enjoy this feeling as I emerge from Stoneshot Lane into the town. At times in the summer, the main street can be congested with daytime traffic, mainly vehicles on their way to and from other places, but often it is fairly quiet and, in the evenings, almost deserted. There wasn't much traffic going through when I arrived late one afternoon. The town was languid, silent except for the screaming of a few swifts racing above the rooftops.

These summer migrants arrive later than the swallows and house martins that share the same hunting skyscape above the town. They leave earlier, at the beginning of August, staying just long enough to rear their young. Like little honorary hawks, they slice through the air on sickle blade wings, snatching insects into their hooked, gaping beaks, constantly in flight except when they visit their nests under the eaves of buildings where they lay and hatch their eggs and feed their chicks. They never deliberately land on the ground. They need the height of their nest sites or a high vertical surface to launch into flight, so, apart from when they are rearing chicks, they spend their lives in flight, even sleeping on the wing.

I once had a colleague who purchased a house with a badly rotted thatched roof that was full of nesting swifts during the summer. He couldn't afford to re-thatch it, so engaged a builder to tile it instead and stipulated that little 'doors' be inserted under the eaves which could be slid to one side when the swifts' arrival was imminent. The builder was disinclined to comply, as he felt the unorthodox finish would reflect badly on his reputation, but my colleague insisted and the doors were duly fitted. I remember him describing the suspense the following spring, after he'd opened the doors, as he lay in bed listening for the swifts' arrival – and his jubilant relief when he heard them. He endured the same suspense every spring, but they always returned within the same two or three nights every April. That was forty years ago when our planet was in better shape, and our roofs less hermetically sealed. Now there are fewer and fewer swifts making it back each year.

Kirkby Stephen's ancient church is a prominent feature, as indicated by the town's name, 'Kirk' meaning church and 'by' meaning settlement. An imposing building with a long nave and the stately proportions of a small cathedral, it is known as the Cathedral of the Dales. The name Stephen doesn't relate to the church or an association with St Stephen, the first Christian martyr, but is more likely to be a corruption of the Old Norse *Vest Idun*, meaning, simply, west of the Eden.

Inside the church there is a block of stone known as the Loki Stone, possibly a fragment from the shaft of an early cross, bearing a grotesquely carved male figure with horns growing out of his head and his arms and legs locked in chains. Once again we are in Viking territory, as he is generally considered to be the

Norse god Loki, although the horns may have been added later by early Christians to make him look like their vanquished Devil. In Norse mythology he was a giant rather than a fully fledged god, but he acted as a kind of clever jester to the gods and was a shape-shifter capable of astounding metamorphosis. It has been suggested that his so-called horns were not horns but the points of a jester's hat. He could be anything he liked, and his transformations included manifestations as a horse, a salmon, a falcon and the ability to change his gender. He was a brilliant prankster who ingratiated himself with the gods and, because they enjoyed his company and the solutions he often found to their problems, he was able to trick them into thinking he was a god too and became known as the God of Fire. He was also very promiscuous and had several wives and mistresses who gave birth to multiple children, one of them being Hel, Goddess of the Underworld.

As time went on his mischievous antics got out of hand and he became increasingly and outrageously full of himself – and malicious. So much so that it was said he triggered Ragnarok, a chain of events that led to the final destruction of the gods and their world. A.S. Byatt, in her book *Ragnarok: the End of the Gods*, sees Loki as a personification of human beings, a species of animal bringing about the end of the world into which it was born; not out of deliberate wickedness but because of a ticking time-bomb combination of god-like intellect, appalling greed, unceasing multiplication of its own kind and a pathological inability to acknowledge the irreversible harm it is inflicting on the planet it inhabits.

* * *

The cloisters in front of the church, built in 1810, once served as a butter market. There has been a regular market of sorts in the town square since the royal granting of a market charter in 1353.

I sat down on one of the benches in the square and surveyed the town. I listened to the swifts' rapturous screams, which were suddenly augmented by the raucous screech of parrots. In many ways, Kirkby Stephen is an austere town. It was a Roundhead town during the English Civil War and still has a plain, no-nonsense dourness about it, so it surprises visitors when pairs of macaws, resplendent in bright red, blue, orange and yellow plumage, unexpectedly alight on chimneys, squawking loudly. They are kept in a private aviary, along with a collection of smaller parrots that are sometimes seen out and about, congregating in trees on the outskirts of the town.

Kirkby Stephen has endured all the usual conflicts thrown up by its history, and many of the buildings bear witness to disputing factions within the community itself. Mostly the dispute was religion versus alcohol. At one time temperance marches and rallies were a regular occurrence in Market Street, and there were fourteen pubs jostling with almost the same number of churches and chapels. Currently there are four pubs and rather more religious establishments, but the people who live here now mostly live and let live, and it is a very pleasant town.

Like any remote, working rural community, Kirkby Stephen struggles with a fragile economy. It has a thriving farmers' mart which is at the heart of an energetic and determined wider agricultural community. Businesses and shops come and go, as do new initiatives, like walking festivals and mock medieval fairs, yet the town battles on, and I think it will win through in the end. It is, after all, at the hub of a veritable countryside paradise surrounded by its nine satellite villages: Ravenstonedale, Crosby Garrett, Soulby, Warcop, Great Musgrave, Winton, Hartley, Nateby and Outhgill, nestling luxuriously in their bucolic Upper Eden splendour; a kaleidoscope of wildlife habitats, including the nationally acclaimed Smardale National

Nature Reserve and three other botanical treasure troves managed by Cumbria Wildlife Trust. The River Eden itself and most of its tributaries are collectively a Site of Special Scientific Interest, recognised on a European level with Special Area of Conservation status; its headwaters around Kirkby Stephen are where it all starts.

This is a very accessible paradise too; a blissfully vibrant, time-layered landscape interconnected with innumerable quiet, sequestered footpaths, bridleways, byways and old railway tracks that radiate from the town and absorb walkers, horse riders and cyclists alike. It always feels to me when I set off to go walking in the Upper Eden area, as the Scottish environmentalist John Muir once said, "more like going in than going out".

North of Kirkby Stephen I followed a length of public footpath by the River Eden through a field known as Edensyde, where in 2009 the town council planted five hundred native trees, including ash, oak, hazel and hawthorn, to be managed as a community wood. The council had purchased the field many years before as an amenity area for the town, but nothing constructive was done with it until someone proposed concreting it over and turning it into a skate park.

It so happened, shortly before I heard this inappropriate suggestion, that I'd received some information from the Woodland Trust outlining a scheme offering free trees to communities who wanted to create new amenity woodland. With nervous anticipation, I attended the next meeting of the town council to suggest that Edensyde might be the ideal site for a community wood. There are nine councillors who were all present at the meeting, which I took to be a good omen. Sure enough, they all shared my alarm about the prospect of a skate park destroying Edensyde's special riverside charm. It wasn't that any of us objected to a skate park per se. There had been support for building one on the much more suitable site originally intended, on a defunct football field next to the grammar school.

For Edensyde, we all agreed that a community wood was a much better idea, and in due course the trees were delivered and volunteers from the Rotary Club and the local Scout Group were soon busy planting them. Conditions were dry in 2009 and the trees were slow to get started, but two or three wet summers since have invigorated their growth and they are now thriving like an irrepressible woodland kindergarten.

I was watching out for the iridescent streak of a kingfisher as I emerged onto the road bridge and glanced down at the river from the parapet. There, instead, was a male sparrowhawk, resplendent in slate blue and orange, gliding inches above the river's surface, head inclined towards the far bank as he searched for prey. He suddenly spotted me and, with palpable irritation, quickened his flight under the bridge to emerge on the other side in a long upward, backtracking, sinuous loop. His sudden appearance caused an eruption of panic-stricken green parrots, which had been hiding in the upper branches of an alder tree. Although it might have been wishful thinking, I was sure I counted nine!

Nine

The Stream Invites
Us to Follow

The stream invites us to follow: the impulse is so common that it might be set down as an instinct; and certainly, there is no more fascinating pastime than to keep company with a river from its source to the sea. Unfortunately, this is not easy in a country where running waters have been enclosed, which should be free as the rain and sunshine to all....

William Henry Hudson, *Afoot in England*

There are almost no Public Rights of Way alongside the River Eden between Kirkby Stephen and the village of Warcop. William Henry Hudson complained that "sometimes the way is cut off with huge thorny hedges and fences of barbed wire – man's dev-ilish improvement on the bramble – brought down to the water's edge. The river follower must force his way through these obsta-cles, in most cases greatly to the detriment of his clothes and temper – or should that prove impassable, he must undress and go into the water."

I was not inclined to put myself to that trouble, not to men-tion to commit a long linear act of trespass, so, a few days later, I drove my car along the lane instead. Pleasingly, the lane crosses the Eden three times en route to Warcop; three good places to stop and stare. I share Hudson's sense of outrage about what was, and still is to this day, a frequently encountered legal prohibition of public access to rivers. Perhaps a systematic campaign, similar to the one that so spectacularly achieved our 'right to roam' over open hill country a few years ago, will eventually win us the right to keep closer company with all our rivers as well.

Two kilometres along the road I parked the car, walked down the byway (Open to All Traffic) which goes to Soulby and stood for a while on the long wooden footbridge that crosses the River Eden, a pebble's throw from its confluence with Scandal Beck. The tributary, a substantial river here, originates from a few tentative trickles draining off the western slope of Wild Boar Fell, and by a happy coincidence there is a view from the footbridge of the fell's distant crouching flank, neatly framed between nearby riverside trees. As the two rivers collide it looks as though the scurrying passage of each maintains its separate rushing momentum, crossing one through the other, swapping sides as they surge under opposite ends of the bridge, capturing an expanse of calmer neutral water in between, before mixing together and settling down as one.

Starting just above Stennerskeugh Clouds, a white moonscape of limestone pavement jutting out from the side of Wild Boar Fell, the Scandal runs down through Ravenstonedale village and on through the lovely hidden valley of Smardale, under the imposing Smardalegill Viaduct. Ravenstonedale has two of the best surviving ancient herb-rich meadows in Britain, 97 per cent of which have been lost in the last fifty years. The Smardale Gill National Nature Reserve occupies 6 kilometres of obsolete railway track and adjacent steep banks of woodland. There are visible traces nearby of circular huts in a Romano-British settlement and the rectangular 'pillow' mounds of medieval rabbit warrens now known as the Giants' Graves. In summer there are wildflowers including spotted, fly and fragrant orchids, bloody cranesbill and wild thyme, and common blue and dingy skipper butterflies, as well as birds such as redstart, pied flycatcher and wood warbler. The Settle and Carlisle Railway goes over a viaduct at the northern end of the reserve and bypasses the quiet village of Crosby Garrett at another one just over a kilometre to the north.

My years with ECCP walking, surveying and managing the improvement and maintenance of Eden's intricate network of public footpaths and bridleways helped me track the wider landscape's scattered topography in my head; its watercourses describe all the twists and turns of the hills and valleys. A river's catchment landscape is a self-contained hydrological unit, complex and confusing, occupying its own extensive but physiographically diverse environmental empire.

Many are badly polluted, and even the apparently clear waters of the River Eden and its tributaries are subject to substantial pollution from agriculture. Thanks to the Eden Rivers Trust, working closely with the farmers, much is being done to counteract recurring problems like heavy grazing by livestock on riverbanks, excess nutrients from fertiliser and livestock waste and careless disposal of chemicals. It is still one of the healthier river systems in Europe, boasting an unusually rich aquatic flora, with more than 180 plant species recorded.

The Scandal Beck supports robust numbers of our indigenous white clawed crayfish, as do several other Upper Eden streams, such as the Belah and, further north, the Lyvennet. The biggest threat to their continuing survival is the larger American invader, the signal crayfish, a more aggressive species brought to Britain in the 1970s and bred in captivity as a culinary delicacy. Within a few years many had escaped, or perhaps been deliberately introduced to the wild, and they are now widespread in many river catchments where they have decimated the white-clawed crayfish populations through predation and as carriers of a deadly fungus-borne disease to which they themselves are usually immune. Even without their presence, the fungus can easily be carried from an infected river to a clean one on an anglers clothing or equipment, so the fishing fraternity's fastidious vigilance is vital.

* * *

Resuming my drive along the road to Warcop, I paused briefly on Blandswath Bridge, the second crossing over the Eden, just south of where it is joined by the River Belah. Further upstream, Argill Beck joins the Belah, and both rivers tumble through a series of steeply inaccessible gills where tracts of ancient woodland have survived since medieval times, supporting an unusually well-preserved ecosystem. Some of the woodland along Argill Beck is managed as a nature reserve by Cumbria Wildlife Trust. Just south of Barras, on South Stainmore, the River Belah cuts through a very deep and narrow gill, which was once traversed by the spectacular Belah Viaduct on the Trans-Pennine Railway between Tebay and Barnard Castle. Demolished in 1964, the viaduct was a huge latticed iron girder construction, 60 metres high and 307 metres long. It was the tallest bridge in England.

At Musgrave Bridge, the third crossing over the Eden, close to Great Musgrave village, I parked the car again and walked along the riverbank on a short length of public footpath where there are some seats, making it a very agreeable place for a picnic lunch next to Great Musgrave's church. The church is dedicated to St Theobald, a hermit monk who died in 1066. News of his death was, no doubt, overshadowed by more pressing affairs in the south of England that year, although he was later made the patron saint of charcoal burners. The present building dates from 1845, but there has been a church on the site for at least eight hundred years. Rush-bearing ceremonies are held here and at Warcop church every summer.

Swindale Beck runs into the Eden just east of the church from its source on the North Stainmore Fells, so when I finished my lunch I decided to walk through the village and pay it a visit. There are wonderful views of two sets of lynchets, prominent ridges on the hillsides, left and right, at the far side of the village where, in the Middle Ages, crops were cultivated on terraces. The beck, more like a river here, regularly breaks its banks, flooding and scouring the fields and depositing piles of shingle and driftwood. The shingle was busy with a throng of excited oystercatchers as well as some fretting black-headed gulls and a number of pied wagtails pattering around on the mud.

Upstream Swindale Beck races down through Swindale Wood down to the twin villages of Market and Church Brough, which are separated by the noisy A66. Church Brough is clustered below its splendidly ruined castle. The course of the beck's journey can be followed much of the way along public paths from a stretch of the Middleton-in-Teesdale road, just below the boundary with County Durham, at the spookily named Deadman Gill Bridge. There might well have been a gibbet there once upon a time, where criminals' corpses were left hanging beside this lonely road for months on end; even today it has a slightly forbidding atmosphere about it.

I returned to my car via a public footpath that bisects the corrugated slope of the lynchet-grooved hill nearest to Great Musgrave. The landowner here is a participant in a 'catch and release' fly fishing scheme that was introduced by the Eden Rivers Trust to provide anglers with financially more affordable access to stretches of the Eden's tributaries. Musgrave Bridge is a good place to search for signs of otters. Naturalists look for their distinctive droppings, which they call spraint. They say it has a pleasant aroma; needless to say I didn't find any; even otters' faeces elude me. I need to try harder – or take up fishing. The River Eden veers off under the bridge skirting north of Little Musgrave, a tiny village just over a kilometre west of its bigger sister.

* * *

Up we go! Up we go! Till at last, pop! His snout came out into the sunlight, and he found himself rolling in the warm grass of a great meadow.

The Wind in the Willows, by Kenneth Grahame

The river remained out of sight as I drove northward along the lane to Warcop. I often drive along here, as it offers a very pleasant alternative to the life-threatening pressures of heavy traffic on the A66 to Appleby. It's an attractive lane where several of the farmers still lay their hedges in the traditional manner. There is no better livestock-proof barrier; unlike a wire fence, a hedgerow can be induced to improve and renew its impenetrable structure for hundreds of years and has the potential, like a corridor of compressed woodland habitat, to create safe cover and passage for an abundant mix of wildlife. Once a hedge has been allowed to grow to a sufficient size, the accomplished hedger starts by cutting away the branches on one side of each tree in line with the hedge.

Each stem is cut through at its base, leaving a hinge of sapwood and bark to ensure it goes on growing, and then laid down on its branchless side at an angle close to the hedge bottom. It is essential that these branches are not laid too horizontally, as some upward slant is needed to allow the sap to rise up the plant. Westmorland purists put in a row of wooden stakes along the middle of the hedge as they proceed, weaving the stems between them and leaving well-shaped specimen saplings at intervals to mature into trees.

I have caught glimpses of the occasional stoat or weasel and smaller mammals like voles and mice scampering from one side of the lane to the other. Identification of plants is tricky from a car, as is the occasional splodge of feathers, which might be the remains of female pheasant, or, more distressingly, a tawny owl hit by a car at night.

A long row of mole corpses hanging from the top strand of barbed wire on the roadside fence along here had worried me for ages. In passing, always in a hurry, I'd estimated there might be fifty, but this time I stopped and counted ninety-seven. They present a pathetically bedraggled spectacle: much more Damien Hirst than Andy Goldsworthy, complete with dripping blood, flies and maggots. I do admit to a slightly anthropomorphic tendency; *Winnie the Pooh*, *Rupert the Bear* and *The Wind in the Willows* all influenced my formative years. I still identify with Winnie the Pooh's naive "bear with a small brain" observations of the rural world, Rupert's surreal adventures in the English countryside, and the intrepid trio Badger, Ratty and Mole doing their valiant best to cope with the naughty Toad. They all inhabit recesses of my subconscious as I try to assert an acquiescent adult perspective in the face of the grimmer reality.

Unlike the gentle Mole in *The Wind in the Willows*, real moles are fierce little beasts, sometimes killing and eating their own kind during territorial disputes. As everybody knows, they spend almost all their lives underground. They mostly eat earthworms, consuming the equivalent of their own body weight in a day and keeping a winter store of hundreds of worms with their heads bitten off to keep them fresh. At just 15 centimetres long and weighing only 100 grams, moles have phenomenal strength for their size and can shovel more than 4 kilograms of soil in twenty minutes with their wide, powerful front paws. They have tiny eyes but very sensitive noses for finding their way around, and their soft, velvet fur enables them to move backwards, as well as forwards, with ease.

Moles inhabit a complex system of tunnels that connect the places they sleep, store food and breed. Displaced soil forms conspicuous heaps when the moles dig tunnels up to the surface. It is mainly the displaced soil, of course, that upsets the farmers, and I don't deny that molehills can cause problems by contaminating silage, hay and other crops and reducing the available grazing for sheep and cows. Moles bring some benefits too, because they aerate the soil and eat harmful agricultural pests such as leatherjackets and slugs. Their spoil heaps sometimes contain shards of ancient pottery and flint arrow heads.

I just wish mole catchers could resist hanging up their gloating, decomposing displays of little corpses. In the nineteenth century mole pelts were sold to the clothing industry. Four million were exported to America annually. One hundred pelts were needed to make the front of just one waistcoat. The humble little subterranean digger enjoyed a moment of glory when, in 1702, the protestant King William III, who had previously deposed James II, his Catholic father in law, died following an accident when the horse he was riding fell over a mole hill. Catholics everywhere raised their glasses in a toast to "the little gentleman in velvet".

* * *

I would like Sheepfolds to be seen as a monument to agriculture. It is a very big project but also discreet because you can see only one small part of it at a time.

Andy Goldsworthy

At the southern end of Warcop village, by the side of the lane, there is one of Andy Goldsworthy's six pinfolds, part of the

Sheepfolds project, containing a sleek, egg-shaped cairn. Built up from the surviving foundation of a derelict fold using a freshly quarried supply of the characteristically red Eden Valley sandstone, the fold and its cairn glow enigmatically in a tucked away corner above Crooks Beck.

The pinfold had virtually disappeared and been forgotten, so it was a little like raising a stone-wall Lazarus from the dead. New stone was used in its reconstruction, and everyone was pleased that a neglected piece of local heritage had been revived – with the added bonus of the distinctive ovoid cairn, like the stamen of a flower representing hope for positive renewal in the future. Unfortunately, part of the pinfold wall sits on what is now a precarious ledge adjacent to a beck, where the ground is subject to subsidence and the wall keeps falling down. There doesn't seem to be much that can be done about it other than regular rebuilding.

Goldsworthy built the six Pinfold Cairns in honour of the Nine Standards; three short of his original intention, but the project had overrun its allotted time and the Arts Council wasn't prepared to give us any longer. Two pinfolds had already been completed at Outhgill and Raisbeck, and I supervised the proceedings at Warcop and the other three at Church Brough, Bolton and Crosby Ravensworth. He had wanted two at Winton and Hartley but was refused permission, even though he'd suggested assembling one with slabs of ice which would quickly melt and disappear, and the other a stone structure buried underground. I had three other possibilities on a shortlist, including one just west of Kirkby Stephen on the road to Soulby, which would have provided a neat completion of the full set.

Ten

Andy Goldsworthy
and Sheepfolds

I need the shock of touch. Nature is in a state of change and that change is the key to understanding. I want my art to be sensitive and alert to changes in material, season and weather. Each grows, stays, decays. Process and decay are implicit. Transience in my work reflects what I find in nature.

Andy Goldsworthy

The Sheepfolds collection was commissioned by Cumbria County Council, and I was appointed as Commissions Manager for the Project in 2000. It had, by then, been running for over four years, starting as Eden Benchmarks did during Visual Arts Year in 1996.

I already knew Andy Goldsworthy, having met him in 1983 at a second-hand furniture sale in the Kirkby Stephen Auction Mart. I'd seen photographs of his sculptures and read about his work, and an article in the local paper included a picture of him after he'd been awarded a bursary to purchase a new camera by the Regional Arts Board. I had liked what he was doing, so when I saw him, I went over and introduced myself as a local admirer. He and his first wife, Judith, who tragically died in a car accident some years later, were very friendly and we went on to maintain a cordial relationship during the remaining months they lived at Brough.

Relatively unknown at that time, he worked as a part-time gardener in return for a rent-free cottage, some modest remuneration and a supply of firewood. He made his powerful ephemeral sculptures with the stones, tree branches, leaves, grass stalks, feathers, mud, snow and ice he found in Swindale Beck Wood. It was the fragility of his work that I admired; the lightness of his touch and his rapport with nature in making abstract representations of nature *with* nature, perfectly synchronised with the changing seasons and climatic extremes.

Photographs of these early structures featured in his 1985 debut touring exhibition *Rain, Sun, Snow, Hail, Mist, Calm*. He lived at Brough for four immensely productive years, making some of his most formative and enduringly repeated images, including a series of gravity-defying stacks of balanced stones gathered from the beck called *River Stone Thoughts*. He reconstructed three of these in the walls of *River Stone Fold*, the Sheepfold at Deadman Gill, where their close confinement now keeps them safe from collapse.

There is another sheepfold downstream at Church Brough Primary School, one of the Pinfolds; a lovely circular fold, perfectly encompassing a tubby and almost cuddly cairn. The children use it as an outdoor classroom and named a new extension of the school building after him. Goldsworthy did some workshops with them and they filled lots of scrapbooks with drawings, poems and comments. My favourite comment was one written by a boy who simply recorded the fact that "Andy Goldsworthy was born in 1956...and he is still alive!" His incredulity presumably came from the fact that the artists he'd previously learned about were mostly dead.

Whenever I walk through Swindale Woods the powerful affinity I feel for his activities is such that everywhere I look I can see the original, but long-gone, artworks in my mind's eye. I'd never seen any of the actual sculptures, only the photographs he took of them, but his intense collages and lines of coloured leaves, dynamic grass stalk squiggles, broken and scratched pebbles and zigzagging patterns of split heron's feathers pervaded my perception of the wood's tangled story at every turn. Every tree-shrouded enclave evoked ethereal reincarnations of his powerful serpentine forms, the ribbons and rings of brightly coloured flowers and unnerving jet-black holes and trenches; spine-tingling impressions of his conical stone cairns and precariously balanced rocks, stacks, columns and spires materialised around every corner.

Goldsworthy modestly denies that his photographs are anything more than keeping a record and creating a permanent memory of his making experience. He is, though, rather a good photographer, and it is the photographs of his ephemeral sculptures, solitary private acts of making, that he shares with us in his big coffee-table books. The photographs aren't artworks in themselves, but they are the nearest anyone gets to seeing the real things, let alone 'owning' one. If I could have kept just one of the sculptures he made in Swindale Wood, it would be one that consisted of four dark brown, mud-covered, roughly spherical rocks, sitting on a bare, wet riverbank, their lumpy somnolence animated by radiating white circles of joined-up grass stalks. The stalks, held together with thorns, sketched a freely drawn line in the air that seemed to spin around the rocks like an electrical charge. Taking the sculpture away would have been sacrilege, like separating a rare wild orchid from the fungi it needs to germinate its seeds. The combination of the mud smeared stones and lively three-dimensional drawing was an evanescent gesture belonging entirely to that time and place – and to Goldsworthy himself in his private moment of making.

Another one was the meandering river shape he constructed by splitting and inverting bracken stems, a form he first made with sand on the beach at Morecambe as a student. He returns to this serpentine form again and again, once on a notably permanent and large-scale using soil and, of course, with some of his dry-stone walls. Although they are not intended to mimic a snake or a river, the analogy is irresistible, as they are both expressions of the shape they occupy by following a line of least resistance through the landscape. Goldsworthy's preoccupation is to seek "a reality of the same intensity" as the one he observes in nature, and he is very good at transmitting that intensity into other people's heads! I often find myself sitting on the side of a hill looking down at the sinuous twists and turns of a river and thinking how much it resembles a Goldsworthy, when I know perfectly well that it is the Goldsworthy that looks like the river. The same applies to the holes he makes when I look at the entrance of a rabbit warren, or his rafts of coloured leaves floating on water when I see sheets of them accumulating naturally in autumn on landlocked pools near the banks of a river.

His primary strength is his aptitude for acute observation. I remember him telling me how he'd visited Claude Monet's garden at Giverny in France, where he made some ephemeral sculptures from descendants of the same flowering plants and foliage that the great Impressionist artist had brought to life with paint on his monumental canvases in the *Water Lilies* series. It made me think that, when he works with colour, Goldsworthy is a modern successor to the French Impressionist movement, sharing their preoccupation with its illuminating power. Paul Cézanne, Monet's more erudite painting contemporary, described Monet as having "only an eye, but my God, what an eye!" In my own explorations of the countryside, constantly in thrall to the dizzying inventiveness of Mother Nature, I find that I look at things with an increasing awareness that I suspect has been heightened by my knowledge of what

Goldsworthy has seen before me with his searching eye.

The colours that so invigorate many of his compositions amaze his millions of admirers; they love them for their decorative finesse, but Goldsworthy denies any ornamental intent and insists that his use of colour is purely an expression of nature's raw energy. He sees the 'prettiness' as an unfortunate distraction. One of my earliest glints of an interest in science was the revelation that the colour of an object is not actually within the object itself but the product of this energy in light, where wavelengths of colour are absorbed by the object or reflected back to be registered by our eyes. It's an optical illusion! It felt like a confidence trick then, and I still don't quite believe that the kingfisher's plumage with its apparently luminous blues, greens and oranges is a fabrication of light reflected from overlapping layers and angles of its feathers.

Shortly after our first meeting, Goldsworthy was appointed as Artist in Residence at Grizedale Forest in the Lake District where he made his ground-breaking timber sculptures, *Sidewinder* and *Seven Spires*, before moving to Scotland and achieving worldwide fame.

* * *

Back in the Yorkshire Dales, all those years before, my tussles with senior colleagues had continued unabated until they came to a head following a chance reunion with Goldsworthy at Abbot Hall Art Gallery in Kendal. He was guest of honour at the private view of a touring exhibition called Artists in National Parks. I was exhilarated by the artworks on display. I especially liked the artists whose practice is literally interactive with the natural environment, such as Richard Long and David Nash, both of them artists who had preceded the younger Goldsworthy. The exhibition comprised a body of work by ten artists, each of whom had been allocated to a particular national park. Andy Goldsworthy was chosen to work in the Lake District National Park, and the exhibition catalogue had a photograph of him on its cover. In the photo he was putting the finishing touches to a half circular structure made from interwoven knotweed stalks standing in the shallows of Derwent Water, its reflection turning it into a full circle like a chunky spider's web. Richard Long had worked in the Dartmoor National Park and David Nash in the Peak District.

The artist appointed to work in the Yorkshire Dales was Garry Miller. I'd been aware of the project right from the start, so when Miller arrived and embarked on his residency I was dismayed when there was no official endorsement of the project, or even a simple polite acknowledgement of his presence. I had decided, not very optimistically, to ask my adversarial boss if he might consider allowing me to write an article about Miller's activity for inclusion in the next National Park newsletter. My pessimism was well founded, and he warned me, with spine-chilling menace, not to get involved with what he considered to be a non-event and an outrageous waste of money. The following week I invited Miller home for supper where he outlined his intentions. He had decided to focus his creative endeavours on Swaledale, collecting organic material as he walked along the course of the River Swale. His technique involved making pictures by placing leaves and foliage in front of a photographic enlarger, shining light through them and producing crisp, bright images on photographic paper. The resulting artwork, in the shape of a cross, was entitled *From Heart to the Head*.

During my conversation with Goldsworthy at Abbot Hall Art Gallery he had told me about his recent interest in dry-stone walls, emanating from a boundary wall he'd made called *Give and Take Wall*. Alluding to a desire to make a wall sculpture in the Yorkshire Dales, he asked if I would be interested in helping him make it happen, including the means to finance it. With careless abandon, I agreed to investigate the possibilities. He envisaged a meandering wall, 76 metres long, with a tree planted in each curve, so my first task was to find a suitable site and a sympathetic, supportive landowner. I'd got someone in mind and, a few weeks later, I went to see the wealthy owner of a vast moorland estate in upper Wensleydale notable for its derelict walls. He was quite receptive to the idea and agreed to let me arrange a visit by Goldsworthy to select a suitable section of wall. He didn't, however, offer any financial assistance. Goldsworthy came for a site visit, chose a conveniently dilapidated wall situated on a slanting bank of rough pasture and went away again, leaving me to make the necessary arrangements.

As no money appeared to be forthcoming from the landowner, my first task was to find some funding and, unhappily, I fell at the first hurdle. The local press, having heard about my fundraising efforts, reported the story in a derogatory and disapproving vein with headlines like 'Wiggly wall grant plea ridiculous' and 'Snake in the Dales sculptor'. Even the Dry Stone Walling Association, an organisation that in subsequent years developed a great enthusiasm for Goldsworthy's walls, derided the proposal because "It wouldn't be a proper wall."

My name was mentioned in the articles, with a strong implication that I was involved in an official capacity as a representative of the National Park Department, when in fact I'd been scrupulously careful to act on my own behalf, in my own time, in a private capacity. I was summoned to attend a disciplinary meeting at the YDNP office and all but hanged, drawn and quartered. My days with the Yorkshire Dales National Park were numbered.

Twelve months after the contentious 'wiggly wall' debacle I bumped into Goldsworthy again at Newcastle Railway Station.

He was on his way to the annual conference of the Association of National Parks, hosted that year by the Northumbria National Park Authority, where he was booked as the association's principal speaker, to give a lecture about his work. Since we'd last met, he had built his wiggly wall in Grizedale Forest and given it the title *The Wall That Went for a Walk,* after a Norman Nicholson poem. Not many people know that this famous wall (which is now derelict) commenced its walk under such a dark cloud of disapproval in the Yorkshire Dales before materialising a year later in Grizedale.

*   *   *

A few weeks after that meeting with Goldsworthy, I resigned from my National Park job and tried my hand as an independent public art consultant. In the ensuing months I picked up a few temporary contracts, notably at Grizedale, where I helped manage the sculpture trail with a range of duties from repairing sculptures in the forest to setting up an exhibition in the gallery. It was an interesting experience, but a hand-to-mouth existence I knew I couldn't sustain. Not for the first time in my life I'd taken a wrong turn, precipitated by an impulsive desire to escape an unhappy work situation, only to find myself in deeper trouble. My predicament this time was complicated by the realisation that public art is something that mostly happens in urban areas and I was deeply, immutably attached and committed to a rural lifestyle. Nature conservation had been my passion since early adulthood, along with an evangelistic compulsion to promote the conservation message, and my vocation was the broader sweep of countryside interpretation. I believe that artists should be recruited alongside ecologists, naturalists and environmentalists to encourage people's more profound engagement with nature and their active support in looking after it.

ANDY GOLDSWORTHY AND SHEEPFOLDS

My self-esteem was at an all-time low and my prospects of finding paid employment in countryside management again were ominously bleak – in the UK as a whole, let alone in Cumbria. Then, just as I was beginning to succumb to feelings of despair, an advertisement appeared in the *Cumberland and Westmorland Herald* inviting applications for a Countryside Projects Officer post with the East Cumbria Countryside Project. It seemed too fortuitous to be true, and I was inclined not to apply, so deflated was my confidence. But I did apply, and when I actually received an invitation to go for an interview I was petrified. On paper, I knew, my sanitised curriculum vitae ticked all the relevant boxes, but how was I going to explain the reality of my frailty in the flesh?

I arrived on the day of the interview convinced that a long and tortuous ordeal would culminate, at the last excruciating minute, in inexorable rejection. It did prove to be a long and tortuous ordeal and I was an inarticulate wreck throughout the day, resigned to my expectation that I wasn't going to be offered the post – and I very nearly wasn't. As it transpired Isobel Dunn, the project leader, had come to my rescue, apparently asserting her authority over other members of the interview panel who had argued against appointing this misguided miscreant. Much later that evening Isobel telephoned and offered me the job; she had a liking for maverick and eccentric non-conformists.

And so, with infinite relief and pride, I became a member of a whole gang of eccentric, non-conformist mavericks. I suspect she also had sympathy with my ideas about art and environmental interpretation. She didn't live long enough to see the start of Eden Benchmarks, but I think she would have approved and I'm sure she would have liked Andy Goldsworthy's Sheepfolds.

Eleven

Long Live the Weeds

A brown little face, with whiskers. A grave round face, with the same twinkle in its eye that had first attracted his notice. Small neat ears and thick silky hair.

Mole's impression of Ratty in *The Wind in the Willows*, by Kenneth Grahame

I enjoy visiting Warcop; I had some happy times there years ago, when I forged close links with the parish council and helped its members transform a wet field next to the village green into a wooded nature reserve, complete with a living willow tunnel maze. The councillors were some of the friendliest I'd ever met and amazingly enthusiastic in support of my efforts, as they were again when I approached them about the proposal to have Andy Goldsworthy rebuild the Pinfold and construct the cairn.

Although Warcop parish is so closely associated with the army barracks and military firing ranges, the village is quite separate and has many of the historical attributes of a typical Cumbrian village. These include a village green with a maypole, a lovely old church, a lively primary school, quaint stone cottages and the annual spectacle of a rush bearing ceremony, when a procession of girls wearing floral crowns and boys carrying rush crosses proudly parades along the main street.

I have mixed feelings about the army's presence; it has a barracks just east of the village, and the 9,700 hectares of the Warcop

Training Area beyond are mostly closed to the public and have been since 1942. But, from a nature conservation point of view, the restrictions give a whole new meaning to the Ministry of Defence. Situated within the North Pennines Area of Outstanding Natural Beauty, over two-thirds of the area is part of the Appleby Fells Site of Special Scientific Interest as well as being in the North Pennine Moors Special Protection Area and the Moorhouse and Upper Teesdale Special Area of Conservation.

The Army takes its wildlife protection responsibilities on the land it has requisitioned very seriously and devotes considerable time and resources to ensuring that conservation management is sympathetically integrated with military training requirements. Habitats like blanket bog, calcareous grassland and limestone pavement are safe from excessive agricultural demands. Rare alpine and sub-alpine flora, red squirrels, black grouse, skylark, linnet, reed bunting, great crested newts and various species of bats and butterflies, all but lost in other parts of the country, have a safe haven here. Thousands of trees have been planted by the Woodland Trust, owl boxes and bat roosts provided and wetland and watercourses extensively restored, along with their naturally occurring waterside vegetation.

Best of all, the really good news is that 'Ratty' is back. The name is a misnomer, of course, the consequence of a water vole's superficial, buck-toothed resemblance to the ubiquitous brown rat. The water vole population has plummeted in the last twenty years throughout the UK. In 1990 there were seven million, but their numbers have decreased by a catastrophic 90 per cent since then. Due to widespread persecution, often because they are mistaken for rats, aided and abetted by habitat degradation and loss, conifer plantations, pollution from farming and sewerage and, not least, predation by escalating numbers of American mink, water voles have become Britain's fastest declining mammal.

They had disappeared from lowland areas almost before anyone noticed, and nobody thought to look for them in the harsher conditions of the uplands. Then several hill-dwelling colonies were found around Alston Moor, one of which extends down Hartside to Renwick below the Eden catchment's eastern flank. A partnership between Cumbria Wildlife Trust, Eden Rivers Trust and the Ministry of Defence snapped into action, taking advantage of the voles' prolific breeding cycle, which spans the period from early spring to late autumn. During this time each female gives birth to approximately thirty babies, six or so at a time. This serial productivity is partly stimulated by the prospect of high mortality rates every winter. The participating naturalists collected the weakest and most vulnerable last litters, and these were incubated in captivity to provide a nucleus of adult breeding stock. In the summer of 2007 more than seventy were placed in 'soft release' enclosures, well provided with food and bedding, around the lower slopes of the Warcop army training area and left to burrow their way out to freedom.

I hope they are doing well and their population is proliferating; they seem unperturbed by the incessant *crash, bang, wallop* of artillery, happily sharing muddy, water-filled ditches with gun-toting commandoes in camouflaged attire. There is every chance that 'Ratty' and his expanding family will pick up a few useful tips on guerrilla tactics, preferably without lobbing grenades, on how to evade their enemies and find safer havens for themselves across the whole of the Eden catchment.

* * *

On foot again, two or three weeks later, I strode through Warcop village down to Warcop Old Bridge and re-joined the River Eden. The lovely, arched stone bridge is called 'old' for good reason: it has survived since the sixteenth century and is the oldest of all the bridges along the Eden. I like its narrowness; a tight squeeze for big, four-wheel-drive cars and tractors but, at the top of its triangular 'cutwaters', designed to deflect the full force of the river there are neat, squared-off recesses in the parapets where pedestrians can stand and avoid having their toes run over.

In the aftermath of a day's heavy rain, the river was displaying a more aggressive air, and its torn and battered banks bore the marks of a concerted and violent attack. The sun was shining as I parted company with the river once more to walk the public bridleway bound for Sandford and Little Ormside. The first stretch has been surfaced with thick concrete as part of an access road, forking off to a farmstead in another direction, leaving the bridleway to continue along a rough cobbled track. Hemmed in on both sides by the tall, spiralling trees of feral hedgerows, luxuriant in diverse layers of new green leaves, it felt like a woodland ride.

The age of a hedge can be calculated by counting the number of tree species and shrubs in a 30-metre section and then multiplying the total by a hundred. The variety of trees along here includes blackthorn, hazel, hawthorn, sycamore and ash, indicating an age of at least five hundred years. The hawthorns were festooned with creamy clots of blossom, and a late spring was making up for lost time with a profusion of wildflowers all arriving at once. The garlic was now in full flower everywhere, its spiky white blooms competing with the softer demeanour of bluebells and red campion. Cascades of purple and golden water avens, bright blue forget-me-nots, purple bugle, ochre yellow buttercups, lilac-hued vetches and green and yellow crosswort frothed around stems of brilliant white greater stitchwort and cow parsley.

A spotted flycatcher was fluttering in and out of the hedge from a favourite vantage point, catching a succession of flies one by one from the air, before disappearing to feed its secret nest of fledglings. A flycatcher's back-and-forth sallies, combined with shape and general behaviour, are instantly recognisable; bird-watchers call this their 'jizz', which may derive from the word 'giss', a World War II fighter pilot's acronym for "general impression of size and shape".

Coincidentally, at that instant, my peace was shattered by a sudden clatter of machine-gun fire and the thunderclap of deto-nating missiles resounding across the simulated killing fields on Warcop's army range. Feeling like a fugitive on the run, I peered through a gap in the hedge at a gridlocked line of lorries on the A66, visually underscoring the sounds of battle, yet eerily silent, creeping along at a funereal pace as the invisible bombardment behind it raged.

The cobbled surface of the bridleway gives way to a short length of grassy track opening out along the top edge of a wide sloping field, where the hedge on one side of the track has been removed, overlooking a recently excavated and geometrically precise lake, busy with groups of restless, quacking ducks. One autumn day years ago, I counted an assortment of more than five hundred grazing geese. The scene resembles, on a miniature scale, the kind of landscape that must have existed everywhere before human dominion over nature really got out of hand and every square centimetre of standing water and marsh was drained to 'improve' the land for agriculture.

Along with indigenous woodland, freshwater habitats provide essential life-support systems for the majority of our native wild plants and creatures. They must also have kept surplus water more contained and helped to avoid the devastating flooding, which has become such a problem in our twenty-first century. Gerald Manley Hopkins, the nineteenth-century Jesuit priest and poet, was an early champion of wild places. He expressed his concern with foreboding in his poems, including in this, 'Inversnaid':

LONG LIVE THE WEEDS

What would the world be, once bereft
Of wet and wilderness? Let them be left,
O let them be left, wildness and wet;
Long live the weeds and the wilderness yet.

The land to the west, north and south is now an uninterrupted tract of irregular parcels of land, hemmed in by hedges, walls and barbed-wire fences. Fields as we know them today were mostly laid out between 1750 and 1850. Prior to that period, much more open lowland commons predominated. Not a wilderness, but a compromise that was compatible with nature. Local people were allowed to graze their animals, dig peat, turf and clay, cut bracken for animal bedding, reeds and heather for thatching their houses and coppice trees for firewood and miscellaneous joinery. They could catch fish in the ponds, tarns and ditches, trap rabbits and hares, collect nuts and berries and wander freely without fear of trespassing. They would, of course, be considered poor by today's standards and had to obey all sorts of rules and regulations, but these were imposed to protect their individual rights and sustain the rich and diverse wildlife environment that, if they showed it respect, would go on providing them with everything they needed. In much of England, wholesale imposition of lowland enclosure legislation by a government of landed gentry and their wealthy landowning supporters did away with both the commoners' meagre privileges and the abundance of wildlife.

Despite my self-confessed anthropomorphism and frequent rants against the indiscriminate control of predators by deluded members of the shooting fraternity, I am not opposed to responsible shooting. The formation of the lake here was, I suspect, probably motivated by someone's desire to shoot wildfowl, and most of the older woods we still have in the countryside are kept mainly because the landowners concerned, and their paying guests, enjoy shooting pheasants. Many hedgerows are tolerated solely for the partridges they accommodate. We probably wouldn't have anything like the diversity of wildlife habitats if it wasn't for the shooting fraternity, but I abhor the barbaric persecution of hawks and mammals that invariably accompanies game-rearing activity and continues to threaten predatory wildlife with extinction.

I made my way, just across the river from Sandford village, through a busy farmyard, noisy with shouting men, barking dogs and baying cattle and, with some relief, plunged into the welcoming, tranquil green embrace of Tricklebanks Wood. The rain had eased off and the sun's sparkling light filled the air with a scintillating clarity. The path climbs along the top edge of the wood, squeezed between a hedge and a straggling line of regenerating blackthorn scrub. It's a pleasant mixed wood, much of it planted about twenty years ago, with a lovely shimmering sweep of bluebells, randomly ornamented around the edges with pignut, dog's mercury, bracken and a few lords and ladies, their green hoods unfurling to reveal slightly disquieting purple spikes. I came out at the top end of the wood into an open landscape of rolling, newly cut silage fields pungent with the stench of recently applied slurry. This is cattle country. I could just see the River Eden slipping along the bottom of the valley, parallel with the line of lorries beyond, still gridlocked along the A66, beneath the towering, glowering ridge of the Pennines. An expansive area of silver caught my eye; for a second I thought it was another lake before realising it was row upon row of polythene strips stretched over a recently cultivated field.

The bridleway here reflects the intensive agricultural regime, with the hedges long gone, and a paucity of wild plants. There are some hopeful-looking woods on the far side of the silage fields to

Below: Long Meg and Her Daughters, an ancient stone circle near Little Salkeld. *Photo © Val Corbett*

The Eden Valley is home to nature reserves that help to protect endangered wildlife, including the curlew. *Photo © John Stock*

Another species under threat, but still protected in the Eden Valley: the red squirrel. *Photo © John Stock*

Global Warming, by Anthony Turner, at Rockcliffe.
Photo © Val Corbett

One of six pinfold cairns by Andy Goldsworthy in the Eden Valley.
Photo © Barry Stacey

Overleaf: Salt marsh on the Solway Firth. *Photo © Val Corbett*

the west, and some wet, sedge-friendly fields in the vicinity of the river. A lone buzzard drifted overhead and was suddenly attacked by a pair of curlew, fearful of it taking a hungry fancy to their vulnerable chicks. Further on, the track is hedged again and the grass verges are alive with pink campion, germander speedwell and crosswort.

The crosswort was everywhere growing in profusion. I love the little wreaths of acid-yellow flowers, held securely in the cruciforms of its lime-green leaves, divided neatly at intervals along the stem. It has a subtle scent and provides bees and other insects with copious quantities of pollen and nectar. The 'wort' part of its name accords with an ancient belief that many plants possessed medicinal properties. Some of them do, in sound scientific terms, providing another good reason for conserving wild plants, but in the old days it was simply the shapes in plants that indicated their potential healing powers. The cross-shaped leaves of the crosswort were enough to convince early Christians that it could be used to treat wounds, especially internally when crushed and taken with a little wine, against ruptures.

Alcohol seems to have been an essential ingredient in many plant-based remedies. Greater stitchwort was also used and said to relieve a stitch in the side or any sudden stabbing pain. An association with elves, however, gave it a slightly sinister edge, as it was believed that stitches in the side and stabbing pains were 'elf-shot' and caused by the elves in the first place.

There are a vast range of wild plants whose English names come from their use in primitive medicine and many more from their value as food. Pignut, sometimes called earthnut, has edible tubers that free-ranging pigs used to eat and were also dug up for human consumption. Conversely there are many wild plants that are poisonous; the innocuous-looking dog's mercury was used as an enema, but is also poisonous and 'dangerously purgative';

the autumn berries of the much more ostentatious lords and ladies are poisonous; it has many regional names reflecting both its phallic appearance in the spring and its perilous tendencies; needless to say it was considered to be an aphrodisiac and many of its names, such as cuckoo pint, wake robin and, rather shockingly, priest's pintle, reflect the fact that its innocuous tubers were eaten for that purpose. Orchid tubers were ingested for the same reason, the Latin name orchis meaning 'testicles' because of the shape of their double root tubers.

Whatever the origin of these fascinating English folklore-generated names, I find them easier to remember than their scientific ones. I know the latter make more consistent, universal sense, not least because the English names vary from county to county, the same name frequently applying to dozens of different plants and individual plants having dozens of different names. These days *Arum maculatum* is mostly known as lords and ladies, but at one time it had more than a hundred names in different parts of the country. Such attention to detail certainly bears witness to the comprehensive familiarity of wild plants in rural communities, which later became the specialism of an educated minority.

Many of the earliest botanists were Christian clergymen with time on their hands. Gerard Manley Hopkins had the same depth of botanical knowledge as the plant-foraging, herbalist apothecaries who had preceded him. He added to his knowledge of wild plants, however, with an amazing degree of aesthetic analysis and wrote appreciatively of their individual beauty, as well as the aura they project en masse from a distance. He described his feeling about flowers giving up what he called their 'inscape', revealing through the senses a mystical essence of the natural world which he interpreted as being closer to his god.

* * *

LONG LIVE THE WEEDS

'Tis seen in flowers,
And in the mornings pearly dew;
In earths green hours,
And in the heaven's eternal blue.

John Clare, from an 1873 poem

John Clare preceded Manley Hopkins by a few years and shared his reverential attitude to nature. Clare worked for much of his life as a farm labourer, gardener and lime burner, but suffered from depression and drank too much strong beer. He was eventually committed to an asylum, where he remained and continued writing for more than twenty years, until his death.

Clare witnessed sweeping changes in rural life as the industrial revolution tempted farm workers to leave the countryside for better paid jobs in towns and cities. Farms became mechanised, pastures were ploughed, woods and hedges cut down, marshland drained and commons enclosed. Clare hated this destruction. He was a brilliant naturalist with an astoundingly accurate knowledge of wildlife gleaned from hours of patient observation. His poetry was inseparable from his nature study. He said that he found his poems in the fields and "only wrote them down". George Eliot once remarked that "If we had a keen vision and feeling of all ordinary human life, it would be like hearing the grass grow and the squirrel's heart beat and we should die of the roar on the other side of silence." Poor John Clare must have heard distant undertones of that roar all his life.

Gerard Manley Hopkins and John Clare were both pioneers of the conservation movement who recognised the priceless vitality of nature. They were part of the artistic and intellectual Romantic Movement, which included Cumbria's own William Wordsworth and his friend Samuel Taylor Coleridge. Other key literary figures included John Keats, Percy Shelley, Sir Walter Scott and Lord Byron. They embraced nature, submitting to the full impact of their emotions, yielding to nature's all-pervading aesthetic power.

I am not an expert in their poetry, but I do understand the deep connection the Romantics felt with nature. As a humanist I try to resist the word 'spiritual', but those special moments when I'm giving nature my undivided attention do equate to a 'mind out of body' experience. A sumptuous mass of pink and purple orchids swaying in a grassy hollow, a copper-red fox momentarily taken by surprise in a silent woodland glade, or a pair of bullfinches foraging along a hedgerow fill my heart and head with joy. I feel an emotional resonance that emanates from the elemental forces of nature, and absolute wonderment at nature's beauty. The Romantics believed that too much science impairs the purity of that wonderment, and I'm inclined to agree with them. That may be a convenient attitude for someone like me, who has always found science too much like hard work, but, as the abstract artist Terry Frost said, "If you know before you look then you cannot see for knowing."

Scientific knowledge is, of course, unequivocally a necessary part of the nature conservationist's armoury and perfectly compatible with a sensory, heartfelt appreciation of wildlife. It's just a question of prioritising our subjective enchantment and knowing how to keep our knowing in check whilst we simply look and listen and assimilate our oneness with nature.

* * *

There are only two houses in Little Ormside. The bigger of these is Ormside Lodge, which has an impressive cedar of Lebanon in its garden, brought back from the Middle East, I've read, by a former occupant. To ensure its survival he put the sapling in his hat and kept it alive during the boat journey with some of his meagre ration of drinking water.

Great Ormside is a small settlement of traditional farmhouses and cottages at the bottom end of a cul-de-sac, terminating at the riverbank. Further back up the lane, just outside the village, there is a static holiday caravan park; taken together the village and large caravan park present an interesting, if slightly jarring, juxtaposition of the tenaciously ancient and the tenuously modern. The oldest building, near the river, is a church dating from the eleventh century, with its hefty addition of a late twelfth-century stone tower and nave and its seventeenth-century roof timbers and furnishings. Along with war and agriculture, religion is one of the cornerstones of our cultural heritage, and churches resonate with a mix of architecture, art and atmosphere that embodies so much of human history.

A church was at the centre of community life, not only as a place of worship, but also to provide a safe refuge when gangs of belligerent off-comers were at large. At such times the church bells were sounded and the community gathered within the relative safety of the church tower. Local villagers' vulnerability to hostile invaders continued for hundreds of years. Outbreaks of fighting between England and Scotland caused havoc in this area, and Eden villages were susceptible, right up to the end of the sixteenth century, to disruptive incursions by Scottish raiders and the murderous family clans known collectively as the Border Reivers, who lived on both sides of the border.

Even as Reiver activity subsided, the English Civil War broke out and Oliver Cromwell's New Model Army attacked churches and castles to enforce his puritan values. They pulled down and smashed a stone cross from the top of the rather grand set of steps by the road junction here. At some much later date, a sycamore tree was planted in its place. It fills the void like a serene, green phoenix. I stopped for a picnic lunch beneath its outstretched branches and marvelled at the peace and tranquillity of Ormside today.

In the early years of my working life I was a National Nature Reserve warden in Wiltshire with the Nature Conservancy, the Government's wildlife agency at the time, and I spent numerous weeks every winter felling sycamore trees to restore and revitalise oak and ash woodland. Sycamore is an invasive species which, as is well known, propagates itself by sending out thousands of airborne seeds on tissue-thin wings. Introduced to this country in the sixteenth century, or possibly earlier, from south-east Europe, it spreads easily into existing indigenous woodland, grows quickly and suppresses the regeneration of native trees. Now more widespread in the UK than any native tree except ash and hawthorn, it is disliked by naturalists because, despite having been here for at least five hundred years, it contributes little to insect species diversity. Compared with the hundreds of species feeding or breeding on oak, birch and willow, only nineteen species have been recorded as being associated with sycamore. Its saving grace, however, is that it makes up for this shortfall by attracting huge numbers of insects from within that limited species range, and these provide a significant food source in the spring and summer for insect-eating birds.

The track opposite the sycamore tree in Ormside, made available by the landowner as a permissive route, leads to one of the few prolonged sections of public path alongside the river. I was so much looking forward to spending some time walking by the river again. The path was part of my 'Discover Eden' Appleby, Hoff and Great Ormside route.

The hedges were bright with the fragile, pale pink blooms of dog rose bushes and the dense creamy umbrellas of elder trees, which were coming into flower after the hawthorn blossom had finished. The path goes under the Settle and Carlisle Railway, just along from where the Ormside Viaduct crosses the River Eden and leads down into a wooded gill called Jeremy Gill. I was resuming my walk almost a month after the day I stopped to picnic under the sycamore tree, and the late spring had been overtaken by advancing summer. Day to day I walk with my dog along the footpaths and bridleways around Kirkby Stephen, including the nature reserves and a few other secluded locations where the fauna and flora is considerably more prolific but there are fewer people.

The steepness of Jeremy Gill has ensured the survival of a mature mix of broadleaved trees, supplemented by a few new saplings planted in protective grow tubes, forming a sheltering green bowl that replicates the feeling of a deep forest enclave. I lingered, hoping for the arrival of something interesting, and, just as my patience started to wane, a hare materialised. Keeping very still works wonders when watching wild fauna. The hare bounded out of the undergrowth and onto the path, where it stopped and sat with its back to me, seemingly oblivious to my presence. To avoid detection hares usually lie close to the ground with their long ears flat across their backs, but this one was sitting bolt upright with its alert ears held vertically, like furry antennae. It was a hot, sultry afternoon and our shared sanctum was intimate, tranquil and cool. Hares have an inexplicable detachment about them, as if they have just descended from another planet. Superficially they resemble rabbits, although they are actually quite different, with a manic, haunted look in their chestnut brown eyes, and their long-legged, muscular bodies built for sprinting at 65 kilometres per hour.

The hare soon detected my presence, staring askance at me for a while, before scampering off into the undergrowth. Hares have good reason to be nervous: their numbers have gone down by 80 per cent since 1900.

THE STREAM INVITES US TO FOLLOW

As I walked on, I was pleased to see two of Pip Hall's bronze panels still surviving, intact on their posts, one depicting images from Viking mythology and the other an illustration of orchids. The path traverses the top ridge of a steep section of wooded riverbank, and I was greeted by the welcome sight of common spotted orchids rising above the long grass, along with red clover, buttercups and meadowsweet. As I stood there I was joined by three men from Ilkley in full hiking gear. They had noticed the bronze panels, so I explained their context in relation to the Discover Eden project and the fact that Pip Hall, who had designed the panels, was the same artist who carved the lettering on the Poetry Path stones at Kirkby Stephen. Not only were they familiar with the Poetry Path, but also with another poetry-inscribed stone on their home territory of Ilkley Moor, which I informed them was also carved by Pip for the poet Simon Armitage. One of a series called Stanza Stones, along a 76-kilometre trail across the South Pennine watershed between Marsden and Ilkley, the poem is called 'The Beck Stone'. It is the only letter carving Pip has done standing for interminable hours knee-deep in water.

The three ramblers went on their way and I stood for a while longer, listening to chiffchaffs repeating their name over and over again – the first I'd heard since starting my journey. The dense scraggy woodland down to the river looked dark and inhospitable, but was evidently acceptable to the chiffchaffs. A flight of steps descends to the river halfway along the wood. Lack of maintenance has rendered them useless, and walkers have trodden a slippery but safer route alongside. At the bottom, the path continues closer to the river, which was flowing almost imperceptibly, like a film of water sliding over glass, reflecting a clear blue sky and the tree-lined banks on either side. The overhanging trees provide the river with valuable shade, keeping it cold and well oxygenated and adding nutrients and cover for invertebrates when their leaves and branches fall into the water. Insects are a vital source of food for so many river creatures both above and below the water surface.

The path comes out of the wood into a succession of fields where the riverbank is fenced off to prevent cows and sheep encroaching on the river. The approach to Appleby is one of bucolic perfection where the farmland has an almost park-like appearance, with a scattering of large standard trees in the fields, including a handsome copper beech. The last bronze panel, a portrait of Lady Anne Clifford, has been torn off its post, a casualty of urban fringe vandalism.

I emerged in the shadow of the river's steep western bank, with Appleby Castle peeping over the top, and crossed the concrete footbridge to the lower ground on the other side, where there is an old watermill known as Bongate Mill. The present bridge replaced an older bridge built to commemorate Queen Victoria's Golden Jubilee. The Eden regularly fulfils T.S. Eliot's description of a river being "a strong brown god" as it approaches Appleby, running amok like a raging Old Testament prophet, thrashing with ruthless regularity everything in its path, including Bongate Mill. Maybe it's trying to tell us something. The lovely old watermill, now a private house, originally had three identical waterwheels, parallel within the building, on three separate shafts. Each was 5 metres in diameter and a metre wide, set between sandstone axle supports. The mill was rebuilt in 1838 after all the vibrating and shaking it must have suffered, exacerbated by the seething river in flood and incessant infiltration of its waterlogged foundations.

Twelve

Appleby-in-Westmorland

Let's join hands and contact the living.

Ronnie Scott, saxophonist and jazz club owner

For twenty years, Neil Ferber, sculptor and long-time resident of Appleby's Bongate Mill, organised an annual jazz festival in the field opposite the mill. He erected a spacious white marquee for the duration of an extended midsummer weekend, with the bandstand at one end, a bar at the other and neat rows of seats in between. A well-stocked food tent stood close by, furnished with comfortable chairs and tables. I love contemporary jazz and attended the festival every year.

A folk music enthusiast of my acquaintance used to tease me by insisting that "jazz musicians play all the wrong notes". Although she meant her remark to be disparaging, I quite liked it. I love all the 'wrong' notes. Jazz musicians revel in the joyous, spontaneous celebration of the moment, and some of the notes that sound wrong to the uninitiated are a synthesis of jittering forays of atonal notes interwoven with exquisite talent. They animate the complex development of harmonies through virtuosic improvisation. Whitney Balliett, the New York jazz critic, called it simply "the sound of surprise".

There is no distinction between composition and performance for improvisational jazz musicians. They play together with an almost telepathic empathy that also facilitates their creative individuality as soloists. Tensions between discipline and freedom, constraint and release, form and chaos are exploited to maximum effect in a musical language that has become a universal force for ethnic and cultural unity. Richly imbued with a restless energy, contemporary jazz is constantly evolving, assimilating aspects of classical, pop and every other genre it encounters, yet always mindful of its history and the courage of its early African and African-American forebears in defiance of their suppression.

Sadly, my folk music-enthusing acquaintance's incomprehension is shared by the majority, and modern jazz is notable by its absence in music venues and on radio and television. Jazz fans, particularly in Britain, remain a small, eccentric minority; but when a few of us come together at festivals like the one that used to take place here, we are an audience like no other, locking into an intuitive alliance with the musicians, often punctuating their performances with impulsive whoops, shouts and bursts of ecstatic applause.

The riverside location at Bongate was idyllic and the river's journey analogous to the music, flowing freely, rebellious and unpredictable, exploratory at every juncture, gently reflective at one moment and dangerously recalcitrant the next, but always irrepressible and sublime. I have to go a lot further afield these days to find comparable little gatherings of my fellow jazz conspirators, their eyes tight shut in a state of sonically induced bliss. Nice!

Barbara Hepworth was one of the first sculptors to talk about wanting to inhabit the landscape with her sculptures, and Joss Smith's *Primrose Stone*, perched on the riverbank here, does so with the compliant aplomb of King Canute, regularly withstanding deep submersion by the river. Shaped from a nine-tonne block of St Bee's sandstone, it looks like a roughly, even carelessly, hewn chunk of rock from behind. Its front elevation, hollowed out like a bowl, comes as a pleasant surprise, expanding with its precisely incised petals, a bee's eye view of the much-loved first rose of spring. Like a Stone Age satellite dish, it embraces the sitter, drawing in and concentrating the sights, sounds and smells of the riverside landscape.

Joss, a gregarious and affable man, makes mainly figurative and representational sculptures that are accessible and unpretentious. He was a joy to have around and worked incredibly hard. I'm embarrassed now to think that I only allowed six weeks for the Benchmarks artists to complete their sculptures, including all the initial research and preliminary development.

Most people enjoy his Primrose Stone, although it does have its detractors. A local painter whose abstract paintings I greatly admire described it as "pure kitsch". Several other Eden-based artists have also been less than complimentary. I had little control over the form the sculpture might take, apart from being a member of the selection committee. When Joss described his intentions, I liked the idea of a simple stone *Primula vulgaris* permanently in flower juxtaposed beneath the castle's towering, snooty grandeur on the opposite side of the river – not to mention cocking a gentle snook at the superior posturing of local artists!

Shortly after all the Eden Benchmarks commissions were completed, I organised a coach trip from Carlisle, with fifty passengers on board, to see all the sculptures. Our visit to the *Primrose Stone* was enriched by the presence of several young mothers and their children picnicking nearby. As we approached the sculpture from behind, the young mothers greeted us loudly with their enthusiastic chorus of approval of the sculpture. As we moved around to the front, we were enchanted to find two of their children ensconced within the stone petals like little flower fairies. I couldn't have arranged it better if I'd planned it. Despite our sudden, rather overwhelming intrusion, they sat tight for the duration of our visit, glaring up at us impishly, complementing the *Primrose Stone*'s naive charm.

The river here is a good place to watch salmon, notably in the autumn, as they battle their way upstream to breed. Atlantic salmon migrate throughout the year, from the sea up to the higher reaches of the river and some of its tributaries, to spawn in late November, December and January. Today they do so in far fewer numbers than years ago, due to pollution from domestic sewage and agriculture, but there are signs that the situation is slowly improving. Female salmon lay their eggs in gravelly scrapes excavated at the bottom of clean shallow rivers and streams. The male then fertilises the eggs and both adults cover them with gravel to keep them safe. The young salmon hatch in April and May and disperse to other parts of the river, where they remain for up to six years, graduating to deeper water as they get bigger, until they are fully grown and migrate downstream to the sea. After one to three years living in the sea, they return to spawn in the same part of the river in which they were born. Once they have finished spawning most of them die, except for a robust minority that go back to the sea and return the following year to spawn a second time.

* * *

Let him destroy my castles if he will; as often as he levels them I will rebuild them so long as he leaves me a shilling in my pocket.

Lady Anne Clifford

Let her build what she will. She will not be hindered by me.

Oliver Cromwell

From the *Primrose Stone*, I walked back over the footbridge and made my way down to the centre of the picturesque town. Once the official capital of old Westmorland, Appleby was granted the title Appleby-in-Westmorland for nostalgia's sake, after government reorganisation combined Cumberland and Westmorland with part of north Lancashire to create the larger county of Cumbria in 1974, and Westmorland was abolished.

Appleby Castle is mostly hidden from view behind its tall, forbidding wall, although it is sometimes open to the public for special events. Lady Anne Clifford, the castle's most famous inhabitant, is an enduring presence still looming large to this day in the town, despite the fact that she died well over three hundred years ago. She was an ardent royalist; loyal to the four monarchs in her lifetime – Elizabeth I, James I, Charles I and Charles II – she more or less ignored the upheavals of the years in between the reigns of the Charles I and II when Oliver Cromwell was waging his violent civil war. Her relationship with Cromwell is intriguing, as they seem to have regarded each other from afar with a modicum of mutual respect, despite their political enmity. Her second husband's turncoat republican allegiance and friendship with Cromwell may have been the reason, but Cromwell evidently admired her stubborn determination. He left her alone to "build what she will" in the midst of all his Roundhead rampaging against the Cavaliers, with their allegiance to the dubious tradition of a debased succession of hereditary kings and queens. Perhaps he approved of her modest and frugal lifestyle; she was one of the wealthiest women in England and yet she dressed very plainly, affecting none of the ostentatious vanity of her counterparts.

Lady Anne's overriding motivation in the few years that remained to her after the war was the painstaking restoration of the huge estate she had inherited belatedly. Damaged in the Civil

War and woefully neglected because of the irresponsible behaviour of her male predecessors, the four castles, as well as several churches and miscellaneous other buildings throughout the estate, were in desperate need of repair or rebuilding. Rebellious tenants, grown accustomed to being left to their own devices, also demanded her attention – although rarely with the drastic outcome that befell Captain Robert Atkinson of Mallerstang.

The approach she adopted to assert her authority over the occupants of her properties and to reinstate regular adherence to their financial obligations was always scrupulously fair and free from rancour. One such payment was a 'boon hen', a custom dating back to medieval times that entitled her to claim a chicken from each tenant in addition to the annual rent. There is a story still told about a particularly difficult tenant who refused to comply. She took him to court, won the case and then invited him to dinner, where the main course served was the subject of their dispute. It is probably the stuff of legend, but there is plenty of anecdotal evidence to suggest that Lady Anne did have a good sense of humour.

The cross at the top of Boroughgate was erected to celebrate the return of the monarchy in 1659, after which Appleby slowly started to recover from the abject poverty it had suffered for centuries in the face of a relentless succession of Scottish raids that left the town in ruins. The buildings on either side, running down the hill to the church, were built in the seventeenth and eighteenth centuries and include a sequestered quadrangle of alms houses built by Lady Anne for widows of the parish, which are still occupied to this day by elderly widows. The Moot Hall, at the bottom of Boroughgate, provides an historically ostentatious meeting place for the town councillors, who every year elect a mayor and indulge in a certain amount of sword and mace carrying and the wearing of ceremonial robes.

Whether all the pomp and ceremony aids their management of the town's affairs is a moot point. St Lawrence's Church, originally Norman, was substantially restored by Lady Anne, and her body is buried next to her mother's in a superior, elaborately decorated tomb.

After a brief inspection of the church interior, I sat for a while in the open cloisters outside, opposite two young women who were devouring large baguettes. A discarded plastic bag lay at their feet, along with the usual detritus of litter, despite the obvious nearby litter bin. I tried to ignore it, but the longer I sat there, the more the plastic bag seemed to assume monstrous proportions in my mind's eye and, as I got up to go, I succumbed to the grumpiness that seems to have intensified with my advancing years. As I picked the bag up and deposited it in the litter bin, I informed them with polite sarcasm that I was doing so to compensate for their apparent ignorance. They emitted howls of protest and the bigger of the two informed me, courteously and patiently, that it had blown off her lap and she had every intention of retrieving it in due course.

Apologetically, I retracted my accusation and scurried away. Similar misunderstandings had happened before, and I wandered around the town for a while feeling contrite and embarrassed. I had that morning been distressed by a photograph in *The Guardian*, spread across the centre pages, showing the contents of a dead albatross chick's stomach: more than four hundred items, including disposable cigarette lighters, toothbrushes and plastic bottle tops. Every year tens of thousands of albatross chicks suffer hideous deaths from swallowing plastic debris brought to them by their parents who mistake it for the fish that are no longer in the sea. They pick it up from a mass of garbage three times the size of Great Britain; the plastic waste of nations, floating in the middle of the Pacific Ocean.

I decided to go back to the cloisters and explain to the woman that this was the reason I'd overreacted to her temporary misplacement of the plastic bag. When I returned, she was standing talking with another woman who was sitting in a car parked nearby. I apologised yet again, described the photograph in *The Guardian* and embarked on a lengthy explanation about the global repercussions of our 'throwaway' society, my fervent concern for which leads occasionally to an overreaction when I see little bits of local litter. She accepted my apology magnanimously whilst her companion observed me with an amused smile from the open window of her car. After a few moments she informed me with a sardonic chuckle that she had guessed I was a *Guardian* reader. So much for the rigour of my tale of global catastrophe!

Compared with the filth and grime of three hundred years ago, modern-day Appleby is very clean. In common with everywhere else in Britain, in the eighteenth century its streets would have been ankle deep in muck, with heaps of decaying household refuse, streams of stinking sewerage, animal dung, pools of festering blood from butchered animals and abandoned carcases left to rot. Unhygienic though all this must have been, at least it was biodegradable. Most of our waste today, the product of a human population that has increased in England and Wales from five million at the beginning of the eighteenth century to 56 million in 2011, an increase of 50 million in three hundred years, is indestructible.

How lucky we are that so few of those 56 million people live in Cumbria – although rather a lot of them do go up and down the A66. Appleby was bypassed in 1981, leaving the town a much quieter place. The River Eden passes under the two arches of the bridge and curls around the top end of the town, looping back on itself, as if reluctant to leave, before continuing its capricious journey north.

THE STREAM INVITES US TO FOLLOW

This part of Appleby is one of the river's favourite localities for periodic flexing of its hydrological muscles, but the day I was there it was a picture of serenity. The only incursion Appleby residents have to worry about nowadays, apart from the river flooding, is the annual gathering of itinerant horse dealers that converges on the town every June: the Appleby Horse Fair. Relatively benign compared with those of the Vikings, the Scots and the Roundheads, this anarchic invasion is nevertheless often marred by incidents of violence and petty crime, and is seen by many as a jarring disruption to an otherwise quiet life.

The event dates back to the reign of King James II, when a market charter was granted to Appleby in 1685, allowing its citizens to host an annual fair for the sale of livestock and merchandise generally; this fair was gradually appropriated by gypsies whose main preoccupation was the buying and selling of horses. The gathering attracts more than ten thousand caravanning travellers, some of whom set up camp on the officially sanctioned site at Fair Hill. Many others stay on local farm fields or simply commandeer almost any spare ground they can find, and every lay-by and village green for miles around is crammed with caravans and vehicles. Some of them still travel in traditional horse-drawn, brightly painted wooden caravans, with extra horses on the hoof, but today the majority prefer modern caravans towed by big four-wheel drive cars and trucks, with their horses in trailers.

*   *   *

It was over a month later when I resumed my journey from Appleby; the summer was fast slipping away after weeks of unusually hot weather. I stayed at home most of the time, alternating domestic and gardening activity, the highlight of which was the rather fraught assembly of a timber summerhouse, with pro-longed intervals of resting, reading and writing in the sunshine and taking my dog for walks on visits to Kirkby Stephen's local wildlife havens.

My most frequent visits were to Waitby Greenriggs Nature Reserve, occupying two short sections of disused railway track on the Eden Valley and Darlington to Tebay lines, which were closed in 1962. The thin covering of soil overlying the exposed lime-stone along the embankments and cuttings there is dominated by blue moor grass and a profusion of lime-loving wildflowers. I measured the progress of that hot summer, week in week out, by their rapid succession. In May there are cowslips and bird's-eye primroses; in June, northern marsh, fragrant, common spotted, fly, frog and lesser butterfly orchids; July, the magnificent globe flower and marsh helleborine; August, devil's-bit scabious and grass of Parnassus and later, autumn gentian. They all colonised the site in the late nineteenth century when the surrounding farmland, untouched by herbicides and chemical fertilisers, was much richer in wild plants than it is today. Owned by the excel-lent Cumbria Wildlife Trust, Waitby Greenriggs was joined up with Smardale National Nature Reserve following the Trust's purchase of the track between the two, creating a wildlife sanc-tuary 8 kilometres long.

My work managing the public path network with ECCP usu-ally confined me to the valley bottoms and I only occasionally ventured up onto the fells. The army range extends as far as Hilton, 4 kilometres east of Appleby, beyond which the Pennine hills have unfettered access for adventurous walking. Public footpaths from Appleby through Flakebridge Wood provide a strenuous circular route via Dufton or Murton. The geology here is complicated but provides an intelligible demonstration of contrasting rock types and formations in close proximity to one another. The craggy crown of High Cup Nick sits at the top of one of the most spectacular scree-strewn gills in England, with the three cone-shaped hills of Knock, Dufton and Murton Pikes poking up in the lower foreground.

High Cup Nick is most easily approached along the Pennine Way from Dufton. It is one of the few places in Eden where I've seen peregrine falcons in close proximity, when a pair swooped out from nowhere, screeching at one another. Peregrines are raptor nobility: they are handsome, aristocratic hawks revered by ornithologists for their awesome speed, agility and power in flight. Although they may have nested here in the past, it is now too busy with Pennine Way walkers. I surmised they were a courting pair out hunting together with a prospective breeding site on a remoter part of the Dufton Fells. The smaller male was cavorting around the bigger female as she oscillated just a few metres above the ground. They seemed not to notice me as they swept dextrously over my head and all too quickly drifted higher into the sky before vanishing across the horizon.

Peregrine falcons continue to be persecuted in the countryside by gamekeepers, egg thieves and racing pigeon enthusiasts. Overall, though, they seem to be maintaining a reasonably healthy population. Part of their success has been the adoption of high-rise nest sites in cities, such as tower blocks and, commensurate with their iconic status, most of the larger cathedrals.

On a recent visit to Lincoln Cathedral I watched on a webcam as a pair prepared a sparse nest in a corner of the cathedral roof, their every move recorded. A cathedral attendant had been extolling the falcons' usefulness in scaring off pigeons, whose acidic excrement causes damage to stonework, as well as being unsightly. After a while I went outside hoping to see the peregrines demonstrate their coordinated pigeon-deterrence duties with a thrilling display of high-speed, celestial supremacy, preferably culminating in a mid-air breakfast-snatching climax. When I expressed this hope to another birdwatcher nearby, we both laughed.

At that instant, just as I was taking my binoculars out of their case, a shower of pungent, globular slime splattered down on my head and shoulders from a tree overhanging the pavement. When I looked up, a pigeon was staring defiantly back at me with a petulant expression of beady-eyed, bowel-relieving satisfaction.

Thirteen

Temple Sowerby

A barelegg'd an' breechesless crew fra the Hielands,
A ragg'd an ruffianly hord.

Anthony Whitehead, from
Legends of Westmorland and Other Poems, 1859

I resumed my Eden journey by driving to Colby, stopping for a
wander along a short section of footpath beside the Hoff Beck
just before it plunges into the Eden. Hoff Beck gushes into life
6 kilometres south of here at Rutter Mill, where the potholing
beck from Great Asby and Scale Beck, west of Gaythorne Hall,
combine in the cascading waters of Rutter Force. Great Asby is a
pleasantly spacious village tucked away at the foot of Great Asby
Scar National Nature Reserve, one of the most extensive areas of
limestone pavement in Britain, laid down some 350 million years
ago under a shallow tropical sea. Common plants such as hart's-
tongue fern, wood anemone and dog's mercury, and occasionally
rarer ones like angular Solomon's seal and bloody cranesbill, can
be found in the shaded, humid fissures known as grikes, which
divide the pavement blocks called clints.

Rutter Mill was first a corn mill, then a bobbin and timber
mill. In 1928 the Great Asby Electric Light and Water Company
took it over and installed a turbine, which for twenty-three years
provided Great Asby and the surrounding farms with electricity.
The power supply was so unreliable that at nightfall residents

switched on the electric lights just long enough to illuminate the lighting of their candles and oil lamps and then, once that was done, switched the electric lights off.

A few years ago, the mill was a café. I stopped for a coffee one morning and sat outside watching a mixed flock of hens, ducks and domestic geese waddling up from the river in my direction. They advanced with intent and paused briefly before charging through the doorway into the café. A few seconds later they burst out again, squawking at the end of the café proprietor's broom in a tumbling agglomeration of dust and feathers. As they recovered their balance and prepared to have another go, he handed me the broom with instructions to wallop them if they tried to gain entry again.

Then he left me to it. I was poised like a conscientious objector on enforced sentry duty. Meanwhile a large cockerel had arrived on the scene, with the potential to foment further unrest, so after a moment's deliberation I drank my coffee, put the broom to one side and absconded.

From Colby I continued along the lane to Sweetmilk Bridge, where a sike of the same name flows down to the Eden. Just west of here are the ruins of Bewley Castle; once a rural bolthole for the Bishops of Carlisle in the thirteenth century, it later belonged to the powerful Musgrave family, until they abandoned it in the nineteenth century. 'Sweet milk' meant fresh milk in pre-refrigeration days, when milk very quickly went sour, so they would have kept their milk fresh by lowering it into the cool depths of Sweetmilk Sike.

Anthony Whitehead, who lived at nearby Reagill between 1819 and 1918 and wrote many poetic *"teales fra lang sin"* in the local dialect, describes a very different beverage given to an unwelcome visitor at Bewley Castle. A Border Reiver gained entry to the castle dressed as an elderly woman in distress. The castle's housekeeper, who was there on her own, allowed the "auld woman" to lie down, and inadvertently looked under her skirt.

> By accident, up her in'd cwoats, gat a peep,
> A pair o' men's shun, an the slops of his britches.
> She just gat a glent at, then teuk the alarm,
> But being stout hearted her wit just bethowt her,
> She'd give a het posset her belly to warm.
> T' auld woman o' t' squab on her back she was snwoar
> While t' housekeeper quickly replenished her pan
> Wi' fat fra the larder – and seun hed it boilen,
> To teem doon her throat, be she woman or man.

Having heard the voices of other Reivers outside, the house-keeper then went up to the castle turret and blew a bugle, summoning neighbours to come to her rescue.

> Then they went an' examined the strange leukin huzzy,
> At t' housekeeper scauded wi' fresh cannel fat,
> An under her gown they seun fand she weare britches,
> Twea pistols, a dagger, buff belt, an what nut.
> Then thet trailed the man-woman far into th' forest
> An buried him snugly an under some trees,
> Though unshrouded or shriven he gat extreme unction,
> At least summet like it, wi' het cannel grease.

I attempted to walk the public footpath from Sweetmilk Bridge to Bolton, but had to turn back when I encountered a tightly packed conifer plantation completely blocking my progress.

* * *

The next day I set off north from Bolton. Andy Goldsworthy has another of his Pinfold cairns in this village. The proceedings involved with rebuilding this were complicated and painfully slow. The first task had been to ensure the site wasn't owned by anybody, as it appeared to have no known owner but hadn't been registered as common land. No owner came forward, so the parish council assumed ownership, and arrangements were made to restore the fold. The council was keen to use two local wallers, who made a good start but were then too busy for a while with other work to continue. Frustratingly, Goldsworthy was away for most of that year too, so not available to build his cairn.

Eventually everything was completed except the capstones on the walls, which Goldsworthy instructed should be cut into triangles in common with other walls in the village. This presented another problem, because the wallers were proposing to use a stone guillotine to save time time and money, but Goldsworthy wanted the stones to be chiselled into shape by hand to avoid them being too uniform. In the end they were guillotined and the job was finished. Goldsworthy was right, of course: they would have looked better with a rougher finish. I had to resolve the impasse, however, as my budget was tight and the Arts Council was impatient to see Sheepfolds finished.

Goldsworthy and the regular wallers with whom he was working often saw things from a completely different point of view. Steve Allen, the lead waller in the Sheepfolds project, was sometimes teasingly critical of the asymmetrical transgressions in Goldsworthy's cairns, but Goldsworthy insisted the irregularities were consistent with his desire to emulate the natural progression of growing shapes in nature. He consciously avoids making corrections that interrupt the flow of form, which he says prevent a cone finding its own shape.

The Bolton pinfold is extremely well maintained by the parish council. Bolton is a remarkably neat village where the village green and the road verges are regularly mown and everything is immaculate. The church dates from the twelfth century and is well worth a visit. I was very taken with the ghost-like stone effigy of a woman dressed in a long cloak, with her hands clasped across her breast, set upright in the wall to the left of the porch. She appears to have a pillow behind her head and was probably originally lying horizontal on a tomb inside the church. There is also a primitive carved skull and crossbones nearby and, built into the wall at the rear of the church, two tiny carved reliefs, one depicting two jousting knights on horseback and the other some indecipherable text. Just down the road there is a row of twelve well-preserved stone troughs, which once supplied the village with water.

From Bolton Bridge there is a footpath alongside the river going to Kirkby Thore and Temple Sowerby. The river runs in a straight line from the bridge between an avenue of trees on either side, and I was relishing the prospect of another long-ish, unimpeded stretch of riverbank walking. My optimism was immediately undermined as I found myself stumbling waist-deep through a battered crop of barley woven into a jungle of Himalayan balsam, butterbur leaves, willowherb, hogweed, nettles and thistles. Barbed wire prevents closer contact with the river, and no account has been taken whatsoever of a right of way. My dismay was alleviated to some extent by a lively population of white butterflies and the occasional small tortoiseshell or meadow-brown enjoying the thistles. I was also pleased to see quite a lot of bumblebees. I'm not complaining about the vegetation itself; the encroachment of willow trees heralds the development of some ever-welcome woodland, but there is no reason why the footpath can't be maintained and kept clear along a narrow line between the riverbank vegetation and the barley.

The river was running fast and had flooded its banks recently, leaving behind layers of mud and deep pools of water. A local man walking his dog, which was hidden in the barley and nowhere to be seen, advised me to follow a field boundary leading to a farm track, but I persevered along the route of the footpath like a jungle explorer and emerged onto the same concrete farm track further on, which led to a row of huge wooden sheds. After careful perusal of my map, I followed the track around the back of the buildings. There are no way-marking arrows to guide walkers through the stark concrete of the farmyard. Hundreds of cows, their heads stuck through gaps along the side of the buildings, munched heaps of silage and watched me with weary eyes as I manoeuvred past a muck spreader filled with their slurry and walked in the direction of the busy traffic along the A66 at Kirkby Thore.

There was a Roman settlement here once upon a time, and numerous Roman artefacts have been found, including several stone altars for the worship of a miscellaneous collection of gods. The Romans tended to hedge their bets and play it safe with a range of gods to suit all circumstances. Trout Beck emerges from under the road at this point to join the River Eden. It flows down from the village of Long Marton, where there is an ancient church containing some stone carvings that appear to be almost pagan in their depiction of mythical beasts with knotted tails, quaking at the prospect of their imminent demise by the sword of a new religion.

After a short, nerve-racking and death-defying dash, inches from the wheels of several juggernauts thundering alongside me, I turned with relief along the footpath leading to Temple Sowerby. Once again the path had been obliterated by another crop of barley; I could see where it should have been and thrust my way through the barley to a gap in the old railway embankment. The gap was full of deep standing water, so I clambered over the top of the embankment and down into more barley. There was still no sign of a footpath, so I shoved my way through the waist-high barley, along the side of the field to the river, over a stile and into a narrow section of ground grazed by cattle. Bliss! The cattle had been very discerning in their grazing, keeping the grass on the path well cropped for walkers but leaving lots of thistles, partially gone to seed and attracting goldfinches as well as bees and more white butterflies.

Just beyond Skygarth Bridge, the River Lyvennet, one of my favourite Eden tributaries, terminates its journey, having travelled via Maulds Meaburn and Kings Meaburn from its source 20 kilometres south of here at Black Dub high on Crosby Ravensworth Fell. The source is marked with an inscribed stone monument commemorating the occasion when the newly crowned King Charles II rested there with his thirsty soldiers and their horses on a hot summer day as they travelled south from Scotland at the tail end of the Civil War:

Here at Black Dub, the source of the Livennet, King Charles the II regaled his army and drank of the water on his march from Scotland. August 8, 1651.

The monument was erected in 1843 by the sculptor Thomas Bland, who created the little-known, privately owned Image Garden at Reagill, filled with his carved stone statuary.

* * *

The footpath along the river ends at Eden Bridge, just northwest of Temple Sowerby. Walking along what used to be the main road through the village is a real treat now that a bypass diverts all the heavy traffic away. It's an attractive village and familiar territory for me, evoking good memories relating to *Red River*, the fourth Eden Benchmark.

When I first walked up and down the riverside route over and over, looking for a suitable site, I favoured a spot opposite Oglebird Scar, a red sandstone cliff on the opposite bank. The landowner, however, refused permission on the basis that the riverbank there is a prime fishing location. Instead he allowed me to site it further along and uphill from the river. The plans for Temple Sowerby bypass were in the early stages when we first installed the sculpture, so it was some years before the bridge over the river was constructed. The sculpture is only just visible from the bypass; it's such a good sculpture that I wish it could have been ten times bigger.

The sculptor Victoria Brailsford is sharply intelligent with an infectious sense of humour and a strong commitment to stretching her sculptural boundaries. Much of her work relates to ecological issues, and she alternates between introspective explorations of the natural environment through drawing, painting, and wood carving and big, bold publicly commissioned statements in stone. She has made several public artworks in both urban and rural settings, including street bollards in Sheffield and a monumental stone sculpture at the Earth Centre in North Yorkshire. She also works in stainless steel, bronze, porcelain and glass.

When she arrived to begin her residency, she had already formulated some ideas on a geological theme. I arranged to take her to a quarry near Lazonby to select some stone, and as we drove there she outlined her proposal. She wanted to use flat layers of red sandstone slabs in some way, but was not yet sure what else to do. She had some thoughts about using large pebbles arranged to simulate a torrent of water flowing over the top of the slabs; we chatted around this idea for a while until, as we turned into the quarry, she exclaimed that she would really like to use stone balls rather than pebbles. Once again, the all-too-short period of time I'd allowed for the residencies reared its head. Carving stone balls by hand would take too long. We clambered around a pick-and-mix assortment of colossal stone blocks, selected three ready-cut slabs and wandered over to the quarryman's office to strike a deal. I was about to go in when Vic yelled excitedly. There, concealed like treasure in a chest, were thirteen big stone balls in a large wooden crate. They were more expensive than the three slabs of stone put together but we bought the lot, as a discounted baker's dozen, amazed by the uncanny coincidence.

The finished sculpture perfectly describes the river valley geology. The stepped slabs represent the sandstone layers, their contours expressive of the light, shade, pattern and form found in the landscape. The balls sit like magnified grains of sand, recalling the origins of the sandstone in the shifting dunes of Triassic Cumbria.

During her residency the National Trust provided Vic with a working space and accommodation at Acorn Bank, just north of the village. The property was given to the National Trust in 1950 by Dorothy Una Ratcliffe, an eccentric patron of the arts, aspiring writer, poet and keen gardener. She was born in Surrey but lived in Yorkshire for some years before moving to Westmorland, when she bought Acorn Bank from descendants of the Dalston family, who had owned it for nearly four hundred years. She thought it fell short of perfection, however, because it wasn't in Yorkshire and she venerated Yorkshire and the Dales. Her poems were written in an awkward parody of a Yorkshire dialect. She was also a champion of Romany gypsies and liked to adopt a romantic version of their lifestyle on annual trips through the Dales in a traditional horse-drawn caravan.

The house stands on a site where an earlier group of more menacing occupants was based, similarly displaced from a heartland in Yorkshire, but choosing rather more dangerous adventures overseas. They were the Poor Knights of the Temple of King Solomon – abbreviated to Knights Templar – which is why a village called Sowerby became Temple Sowerby in the thirteenth century. Dedicated to upholding the Christian occupation of the Holy Land in the Middle East, this powerful and ruthless elite of warrior monks had its main headquarters at a mosque on the site of Solomon's Temple in Jerusalem, revered by Christians and Muslims alike. Dressed in crusaders' white tunics emblazoned with the blood-red cross of St George, they were fearless fighters who believed that dying on the battlefield in combat with Islamist warriors guaranteed them a place in Heaven. Over eight hundred years later it seems all too tragically familiar as the same religious conflict continues around the world. Will we ever be free from the tyranny of religion?

I'm glad the National Trust owns Acorn Bank now. The Trust is a powerful force in the United Kingdom for the conservation management of expansive rural estates that were once held by a wealthy minority, with access denied to the general public. The Trust has only two properties along the length of the River Eden, but owns a quarter of the Lake District, including more than ninety farms and six of the major lakes and their shores.

Acorn Bank acquired the name because of its magnificent oak woodland. Much of the woodland was felled in the eighteenth century by the Dalston family to improve their view of the Lakeland mountains from the front of the house, but there are still some magnificent specimens in the remaining woods behind the house. Crowdundle Beck, springing from Cross Fell, flows through the woods and was once the border between the old counties of Cumberland and Westmorland.

THE STREAM INVITES US TO FOLLOW

A walled garden is well stocked with more than two hundred and fifty culinary and medicinal herbs and plants, and elsewhere there is a pond with breeding newts, a large collection of different varieties of apple trees, beehives, well-tended lawns and copious flower beds. There is also a very pleasant tearoom. The house itself is undergoing extensive refurbishment.

National Trust volunteers have recently rebuilt and restored an old watermill to grind corn after seventy years of dereliction. Crowdundle Beck has been brought into service again, with some of its water being drawn along the mill race to drive the waterwheel. The beck won't have to work quite as hard as it did in the 1880s when three waterwheels provided power for a saw bench cutting timber, the transportation of gypsum from an underground mine at the other end of the woods, and the production of flour.

I visit Acorn Bank regularly, not least because there are lots of different bees, which are fascinating to watch and frustratingly difficult to identify. Penrith Beekeepers Association have four hives of honeybees at the rear of the orchard to facilitate research and help pollinate the apple trees, but it is the wild bumblebees that fascinate me. There are twenty-three species of bumblebee, eight of them being common garden species. The flight of these endearing, rotund insects as they buzz from flower to flower necessitates an astounding two hundred and forty wing beats per second to keep them airborne.

I'm ashamed to admit that I have only recently, late in life, started to take notice of the insect world. I lament the imminent demise of tigers, elephants, cheetahs and orangutans, which are too far away to see in the wild, but their miniature equivalents, many of them just as rare and threatened with extinction, can be observed around Britain in their thousands. There are around twenty thousand British species of insects, which we mostly ignore: dragonflies, damselflies, butterflies, moths, beetles, grass-hoppers, ants, bees and wasps, many with sensational habits and names like leopard moth, elephant hawkmoth, bloody-nosed beetle, devil's coach-horse beetle and golden-ringed dragonfly.

Places like Acorn Bank's gardens provide them with a degree of shelter in a frequently malign wider agricultural landscape. Bumblebees, solitary bees and hundreds of other insects species are an indispensable factor in our own survival. They pollinate the trees that produce the oxygen we breathe, as well as the plants that feed other insects, which feed the birds; a life-affirming cycle of perpetual renewal. The world's food crops are entirely dependent on this cycle, yet we are killing insects with pesticides and herbicides on an unprecedented scale.

Fourteen

Natural and Human History Intertwined

He pass'd red Penrith's Table Round,
For years of chivalry renown'd
Left Mayburgh's mound and stones of power,
By druids raised in magic hour,
And traced the Eamont's winding way.

Walter Scott, 'The Bridal of Triermain'

The next day I drove from Culgaith along the high road to Langwathby, parallel with the course of the River Eden, and stopped halfway to look at the view across to Penrith. The River Eamont flows past Brougham Castle and enters the Eden abruptly 6 kilometres east of Penrith. It is the first of the Eden's bigger tributaries and connects the Eden Valley with the Lake District. Eden's tourism economy would benefit from a closer association with the Lakes, and recognition that two of the lakes, Ullswater and Haweswater, are integral parts of the River Eden's catchment.

Ullswater, the second largest lake in the Lake District, is fed by an abundance of substantial becks pouring in from the surrounding mountains. One of these is Aira Beck, which starts on the eastern slopes of Great Dodd, a grassy, domed mountain 857 metres high. The beck wriggles down the fell to a small valley where Helen Sutherland, a wealthy patron of the arts during and after the First World War, lived in isolated splendour at Cockley

Moor. Over many years she was an ardent supporter of painters such as Ben and Winifred Nicholson, who were avant-garde artists at that time, and poets Kathleen Raine and Norman Nicholson. They often came to stay with her at Cockley Moor, and Kathleen Raine lived for the duration of the war at Martindale Vicarage, on the other side of Ullswater.

The Ullswater Way, a 32-kilometre-long walking route circumnavigating the lake, includes three poetry stones inscribed with extracts from two of Kathleen Raine's poems. The lettering was carved on existing rocks by Cumbria's inveterate carver of poems, Pip Hall. They can be found in Hallinhag Wood, a short distance north-east from Sandwick Bay.

Ullswater is the jewel in the River Eden's catchment crown and the source of the River Eamont. Breaking away from the lake at Pooley Bridge, the Eamont weaves through the flat farmland, rich with historic remains.

Mayburgh Henge, King Arthur's Round Table, Brougham Hall, Brocavum Roman Fort, Brougham Castle and the Countess Pillar are all within easy walking or driving distance of Penrith. Brougham Castle and the Countess Pillar are reminders once again of the magnificent Lady Anne Clifford. The castle was her main residence in the last few years of her life, and she died there on March 22, 1676. Her mother had died there sixty years previously when Lady Anne was just twenty-six years old. She erected the Countess Pillar in 1654 in memory of her mother, at the last place they had spent some brief time together prior to Lady Anne's departure on a trip to London. I have huge admiration for Lady Anne. She agitated with an amazing determination for the right to inherit her family's Westmorland estates after her father's death in 1605, over a period of forty years, despite the seemingly incontrovertible odds against women having any rights at all – to anything.

Women in general were considered to be their husbands' property and had no influence whatsoever in the management of their own lives, financial or otherwise. They couldn't own houses or land or enter into any legal agreements, and even their children were the subject of their husbands' exclusive guardianship. Rare exceptions sometimes occurred within the upper classes when a woman was allowed to inherit an estate if there was no male heir, to ensure that it was kept in the family until a suitable male became available. These immensely privileged women were also unusual in that they had the benefits of an education and so were judged capable of managing the family inheritance responsibly and efficiently.

The Clifford family had a long history of closeness to royalty, one outcome of which was that they were regular recipients of generous royal gifts of land. King Edward II, who gave them the Skipton Castle estates in 1310, had issued a directive that ownership of all Clifford lands should be passed to the direct heir in perpetuity, regardless of gender. Lady Anne's two brothers died in childhood, she'd had a superb education and was clearly very intelligent, so it should have been a foregone conclusion that she would inherit the estate, but her father, George Clifford, the Queen's Champion and one of England's most celebrated piratical adventurers, on the high seas and abroad, thought otherwise and chose to leave it all to his brother. Immediately after his death Lady Anne's doting mother initiated proceedings to contest the will on her behalf and Lady Anne took up the challenge after her mother died, undaunted by the opposition of her rather nasty second husband, several wayward male cousins and that creepy survivor of the gunpowder plot and keen advocate of witch hunting, King James I. It proved to be a painfully long battle, dragging on for most of her life, before she finally achieved a triumphant outcome after all the men had died and she was enabled, at last, to implement the plans she'd held in abeyance for so long, which so revitalised her beloved Westmorland estates.

As well as dedicating the Countess Pillar to the memory of her mother, she also left an annuity of four pounds to be distributed to the poor of Brougham Parish on the second day of April every year. The money was placed on a block of stone known as the Dole stone, which sits beside the pillar; there is still a ceremony held here every April, when money is collected for charity.

When I devised the Brougham and Eamont Bridge walk as part of the Discover Eden project, I was keen to include the Countess Pillar on the route, but the only access available at that time was a short, grassy road verge track in dangerous proximity to the traffic on the A66. I knew the road had been realigned when it was turned into a dual carriageway and further investigation revealed that the redundant section of the original road was still there, leading away from the back of the pillar, screened by trees and disengaged from the speeding vehicles hurtling along the A66.

Joining neatly with the quiet road that leads off the A66 to Brougham Castle and Brougham village, this small piece of road had obvious potential to provide safer and more congenial access to the Countess Pillar, including for wheelchairs. It had been used as a dump for broken concrete drainpipes and posts, kerbstones, heaps of bricks and hardcore, big rolls of rusting fence netting and piles of general builders' debris. Its tarmacadam surface was still intact, so it seemed just a simple matter of removing the rubbish, importing soil for some landscaping to reduce the width of the path, planting a few trees and creating a suitably graded and solid ramped path to the pillar. How wrong I was!

My assumption had been that the old road still belonged to the Highway Authority, so all I needed to do was liaise with its local office to get the job done. It transpired, however, that ownership of the redundant road and all the land associated with it had reverted to its original owner, the neighbouring farmer. Luckily, he proved to be a most intelligent and helpful man, willing to help in any way he could. He informed me that English Heritage owned the Countess Pillar and that he'd met with several of its staff members on a number of occasions to discuss making the road available for public access – to no avail. He recommended that I get in touch with them and also seek planning advice from Eden District Council.

The District Council Planning Officer told me that the old road, despite its tarmacadam surface, was now, technically, agricultural land and not a road, so I had to apply for a change of use. I had site meetings with several different officers from English Heritage, each with distinctly different roles and sometimes conflicting ideas; I had to commission an archaeological assessment; and health and safety loomed large on the agenda. We got there in the end. It occurred to me, once all the work was completed, that the reason Lady Anne and her mother stood together for the last time at the particular location was probably because Brougham Castle's drive started where the pillar now stands. It had probably been the grand entrance to the castle grounds, resplendent with ornate gates.

* * *

West of Brougham Castle, the River Eamont is joined by the River Lowther. Rising on the fells south-west of Shap, it feeds into Wet Sleddale reservoir and heads north, picking up Swindale Beck and a host of Lake District mountain streams that plummet into Haweswater. They emerge as Haweswater Beck to join the Lowther at Bampton, which continues north past Helton, Askham and Eamont Bridge.

From Brougham Castle the River Eamont swerves in a contorted loop before forming a straighter line prior to converging with the Eden. Halfway along it passes below Nine Kirks, a tiny, isolated church originally built in the thirteenth century at the centre of a long-lost village and then rebuilt from a ruin in 1654 by Lady Anne Clifford. Unlike the Nine Standards at Kirkby Stephen, the number nine in this case doesn't make much sense. It could be a corruption of the name Ninian, indicating a link with St Ninian. 'Kirk', of course, is a Viking word for church, still used in Scotland, but I'm still left wondering about the plural 'Kirks'. I visited Nine Kirks, which is a plain, unassuming church, not long after I first started working for ECCP, but I haven't been back since. I like churches as buildings and appreciate their characteristic architecture, but a deep, archaic melancholy seems to pervade the dark fabric of some of their interiors, and a sanctimonious, detached and cold atmosphere sometimes seems to cut them off from the reality of life outside.

As I gazed at the magnitude of the wider bucolic scene, with its resonances of natural and human history intertwined, stretching away into the distance, a wren burst into song in the nearby hedgerow. It repeated the same succession of shrill notes over and over, teetering on its perch in the tangled vegetation as if it could hardly believe that such a loud and penetrating noise was coming from its own diminutive body. Wrens display a wonderful zest for living in their foraging from place to place, filling the air around them with that strident song in a spirit of incontrovertible joy. Their tiny frames make them susceptible to freezing winters, and many die every year, but, although individuals favour a solitary existence, they have developed the habit of roosting at night in large numbers, huddled together for warmth in confined spaces. Up to sixty wrens have been recorded emerging from one small nest box on a winter morning.

Fifteen

Edenhall

I parked the car across the river from Langwathby at the end of the longest-standing temporary metal bridge in Britain and walked along the riverbank to a path known as Ladies' Walk. The footpath soon veers away from the river and ascends the wooded, higher ground to where the fifth Eden Benchmark sculpture, *South Rising*, is located. It was made by Vivien Mousdell, a versatile artist who is deeply sincere in everything she does – her restless creative energy knows no bounds.

All the Benchmark artists enriched my life with their kindness, good humour and remarkable insights into the things in life that really matter, and Vivien got me off to a flying start.

Her sculpture was the first of the Eden Benchmarks to be installed. *South Rising* comprises two carved stones situated more or less at the mid-point along the river. One lies flat on the ground, indicative of the flow of the river to the north, and the other stands vertically, set at a slight angle, with its pointed top inclined in the direction of the river's source to the south. Both stones are red Lazonby sandstone carved into sweeping, rhythmic shapes like the surrounding landscape and chiselled with a surface texture reminiscent of water-reflected sunlight.

When the sculpture was first installed it perfectly fulfilled the expectations of a 'sculpture for sitting' overlooking the river and captured a real sense of place. Vivien shaped the seat stone and placed it in conjunction with its standing companion in such a way that the sculpture as a whole mimics the bend in the river below. There was a clear view of the river then over the tops of the willow saplings, and I had anticipated the trees would be coppiced by the landowner before they grew too high. Unfortunately, that hasn't happened, and the visual connection with the river, which was such a crucial part of the sculpture's conception, has sadly been lost. There is also the danger that as the willows grow bigger, they will destabilise the bank and cause a landslide.

* * *

The path resumes its riverside course down some stone steps, where a section of the neatly delineated Ladies' Walk still survives, leading to a track, which snatches us away from the river across a field to Edenhall village. St Cuthbert's Church stands alone, close to an overgrown water hole called St Cuthbert's Well. Most of the earliest churches were built on, or close to, springs of water often enclosed in wells.

The earliest pagans were devoutly reverential of water, because they recognised the simple fact that streams and rivers were the life blood of their world. Nomadic peoples wandered from water hole to water hole and when they settled in one place their lives revolved around the permanent availability of water. Springs were regarded as a gift from the all-powerful Earth Mother who, pagans believed, controlled birth, life and death.

Water does have something of an unworldly appearance; a kind of ethereal quality in some lights. No surprise then that the pagans were persuaded to switch from the earthly logic of their maternal deity to worship a new sky-dwelling god, and that the objects of their deification were adapted, with water retaining a central role. Christian churches were built on pagan sanctuaries, and the springs they contained continued to be venerated by Christians with much the same reverence as the pagans they were ousting. The wells were dubbed Holy Wells and dedicated to Christian saints. St Cuthbert was an Anglo-Saxon monk who resided at Lindisfarne in the seventh century. There are other wells dedicated to St Cuthbert in Cumbria, notably at Wetheral. In the wild, remote regions of old Cumbria people still clung to an mix of superstitious belief in goblins and fairies living in a twilight dimension where heathen gods still held sway alongside the new god. St Cuthbert's Well is a good example.

A glass drinking chalice decorated with gold and coloured enamels was allegedly found buried near St Cuthbert's Well. St Cuthbert's followers, constantly trying to avoid capture by Viking raiders after he died, hid many of his possessions at religious sites all over the north of England, and Edenhall might well have been one such place. According to antiquarians, the glass vessel came from Syria during the fourteenth century, seemingly implicating those marauding crusaders the Templar Knights, who could have brought it back after one of their incursions in the Middle East. Now in the Victoria and Albert Museum, the chalice was known as the Luck of Edenhall and was originally owned by the Musgrave family, who lived for four hundred years, until the eighteenth century, in a grand mansion in the village. Local legend tells us that the family's butler visited the well one night to fetch some water and disturbed a spritely bunch of fairies dancing in a circle around the sparkling goblet. For some unknown reason they allowed him to take it away, but as he did so they sang a little warning song.

> If e'er this glass should break or fall
> Farewell the luck of Edenhall!

The story probably derived from all that lingering pagan folklore about the protective magic surrounding a precious source of water. 'Luck' receptacles have also been found near Great Salkeld and Kirkoswald.

A stone cross known as the Plague Cross stands by the field gate. Typhoid killed a quarter of Edenhall villagers in the late sixteenth century. Sufferers lived in a camp near the river, well away from the village, and put money into a basin filled with vinegar to pay for food delivered by traders from Penrith. I rested on a bench by the war memorial in the centre of the village, which is bypassed by the main road so that very little traffic disturbs its peace. I'd assumed the village got its name from the Musgraves' mansion which was demolished in 1934, but apparently 'hall' comes from *haugh*, a Scots word meaning flat land by a river. The clock tower and courtyard are all that remain of the mansion.

Sixteen

Beneath Fiends Fell

I resumed the next stage of my journey from Little Salkeld a few days later. The River Eden reaches full adulthood along here and has become a much bigger river, moving majestically through the lush farmland of the middle Eden Valley. There is almost no public access to its banks between Temple Sowerby and Armathwaite, a distance of more than 20 kilometres. As a consequence of this, the second half of my journey was less intimate with the river than the earlier sections had been.

* * *

The UK's public path network, despite all its admirable attributes, does have its shortcomings. It came about as a result of legislation following a 'mass trespass' on private land in the Derbyshire Peak District in 1932. Five hundred ramblers from Manchester and Sheffield marched across the moors, where they met with a hostile reception from a large group of gamekeepers and policemen. This culminated in some violent altercations, and several of the ramblers were sent to jail.

The event, however, attracted such massive popular support that seventeen years later, after persistent lobbying by ramblers, the government brought in the 1949 National Parks and Access to the Countryside Act. This required all local authorities throughout England and Wales to conduct an investigative survey of all the existing cross-country paths in their areas to determine which of them should be officially sanctioned as Public

Rights of Way. Eventually all of these appeared on what came to be called 'The Definitive Map'. In practice it's a vast collection of definitive maps, kept in sets relative to their locality by the appropriate local authorities and parish councils. Its production involved a laborious democratic process, going through several stages, with draft maps being displayed periodically for public scrutiny and consideration.

The problem in the early 1950s was that visitors were few and far between in remote rural areas like Cumberland and Westmorland. The concept of recreational walking, especially in the valleys, was a relatively new phenomenon. Most of the paths functioned as a de facto resource, familiar only to local residents and used for mainly practical purposes. A path's inclusion on the Definitive Map was invariably dependent on a landowner's compliance. There were some who just let it all happen and others who made sure it didn't. Consequently, there are glaring inconsistencies, with some areas virtually overwhelmed by paths crossing and re-crossing fields, which make no sense at all, and others where paths are entirely absent in places where they would have made very great sense indeed, such as alongside rivers. Many of the omissions were on the big estates owned by politically astute men, who were usually members of their local authorities. Better informed than their working farmer neighbours, they could anticipate the future implications of legalising paths on their land and the connotations, as they saw them, for their exclusive shooting and fishing pursuits.

Many similar landowning people were up in arms during the run up to the more recent Countryside and Rights of Way Act in 2000, which came into effect in 2005 and gave the public the right to walk freely on mountains, moors, heaths and downs without having to be on paths. It was dubbed 'the right to roam' at the time, and there was confusion about what that meant, some farmers thinking it included ordinary farmland, which it didn't, and some big landowners in Cumbria insisting it would result in the fells and moors being overrun with "all sorts of riff raff", which it didn't. Most people still prefer to keep to the paths on lower ground.

I've always been fond of a cartoon that originally appeared in the early satirical magazine *Punch* depicting a tough rambler standing his ground in front of a haughty landowner on horseback who had ordered him to "Get off my land!" The rambler asked him what gave him the right to own such a lot of land, and the reply came, "Because my ancestors fought for it." To which the rambler retorted, "Well, get off your horse and I'll fight you for it now." People like me who enjoy wandering around the countryside owe a huge debt of gratitude to ramblers like him, and, despite my griping about the Definitive Map and its omissions, I really do appreciate the amazing network of paths that ramblers of his ilk and members of the ever-tenacious Ramblers' Association achieved all those years ago.

* * *

The hamlet of Little Salkeld has another watermill. Privately owned, it produces organic flour and has an award-winning tea room; I was soon sitting devouring a hearty vegetable soup with a selection of tasty chunks of proper bread in the simple kitchen interior. The café interior makes me feel as if I've walked into a painting by Johannes Vermeer. The water that drives the main waterwheel comes from a tiny beck that is an offshoot of Robberby Water, rising on Cross Fell, the highest point on the Pennines. It and another substantial stream called Briggle Beck feed into the Eden just west of Little Salkeld. When the sluice controlling the flow of water in the mill race is open, an average of 4.55 million litres pours through every day. It must be scary in times of flood.

Robberby Water flows through the spacious village of Melmerby, six or so kilometres east of here, where another sheepfold, which had almost disappeared and been forgotten, was rebuilt by Steve Allen and his assistant George Allonby for Andy Goldsworthy. This particular sheepfold is a wash fold, a two-chambered structure sitting alongside the beck where the water was once dammed regularly with wooden planks inserted into a sluice to create a deep pool, or dub, for washing sheep. Goldsworthy made a sculpture he called *The Dub Stone* by carving holes of decreasing sizes down through the middle of a block of red sandstone, which he had split into layers. He'd made similar receding-holes pieces many times before, with sand and clay as well as stone, and describes them as "going back in time". Placed on the bed of the beck, he'd expected *The Dub Stone* to be permanently underwater, until he realised that achieving this would require the sluice to be shut permanently, with the risk of continuously flooding the road.

The ECCP estate team had reinstated the sluice, and, after rebuilding of the wash fold was completed, Goldsworthy arrived one nondescript overcast October day to take photographs. He was already planning his next book, *Enclosure*, which predominately features pictures of sheepfolds, and the *Dub Stone Fold* was one he was excited about, not least because filling the dub with water activates its own ephemeral kaleidoscope of swirling light and colour. Whilst he assembled a scaffold platform, with his camera fixed to a tripod standing precariously on top of it, I removed an accumulation of grit and debris from the hole in *The Dub Stone*.

Then, as he pointed his camera lens downwards, directly over the hole, I inserted the planks in the sluice, forcing the water to rise. As it did so, concentric circles of red dust within the hole formed on its surface, whilst a scattering of leaves floating on the sky-reflecting sheen of water surrounding the sculpture provided a contrasting, slowly shifting accompaniment. There is a delectable sequence of the photographs in his book, culminating in one full-page shot of *The Dub Stone* totally submerged, captured underwater like a fossil in amber.

* * *

The main road east of Melmerby climbs abruptly through a vertiginous gap in the Pennine ridge over to Alston, the highest market town in England. The ridge is a wild escarpment of rough, stony grassland more than 12 kilometres in length, incorporating Cross Fell, rising to 893 metres at its summit, Little Dun Fell (842 metres) and Great Dun Fell (848 metres). Notorious for its dreadful weather, the whole area is known as Fiends Fell because of the fiendish shrieking sound made by a unique meteorological rotor-streaming phenomenon called the Helm Wind – the UK's only named wind. The wind occurs when a strong and sometimes violent north-easterly gale, most frequently in late winter, accumulates under a heavy cap of thick fog along the felltop before pouring downhill at high speed beneath a rolling band of parallel cloud.

Despite the harsh weather, the fells over this central part of the Pennine Hills support an interesting and important rare flora that survives from the Ice Age. Great Dun Fell is part of the Moor House and Upper Teesdale National Nature Reserve, but is better known for the giant 'golf ball' radar station, operated by the National Air Traffic Services, on its summit.

From the village of Knock there is a tarred road leading to it, which prohibits public traffic from about a mile outside the village. A group from the ECCP was given permission on one occasion to drive up there with a group of council officials for a ceremony in memory of Isobel Dunn, the Project's leader, soon after her death. A short piece of dedicated text had been carved on a rock some distance west of the radar station, and we all walked along a flagstone section of the Pennine Way battling against a wind that grew more severe with every step. As we assembled around the rock it started to rain, necessitating an abruptly curtailed ceremony and a hasty retreat. The council officials trudged straight back along the flagstone path to the safety of their parked vehicles, whereas we ECCP people, who should have known better, sought shelter from the pounding rain and wind in the lee of the ridge.

Fortunately, it wasn't the Helm Wind – but, as the rain and wind eased off, an impenetrable fog descended and we were lost. We'd strayed too far down the slope and ended up walking around in circles. Our only option was to follow a tiny beck down the hill, involving a disconcerting, hazardous descent by scrambling, slipping and sliding until we emerged hours later on lower ground, where we were met by a fell rescue team, called out by the councillors, clambering up towards us. We were lucky that the only injury we suffered was our acute embarrassment.

Seventeen

Long Meg and Her Daughters

Faster than fairies, faster than witches,
Bridges and houses, hedges and ditches;
[...]And ever again, in the wink of an eye,
Painted stations whistle by[...]
Here is a child who clambers and scramble,s
All by himself and gathering brambles[...]
And here is a mill and there is a river:
Each a glimpse and gone forever!

Extract from 'From a Railway Carriage',
by Robert Louis Stevenson

Resuming my walk from Little Salkeld Mill, well fortified by the soup and bread, I set off to where the river comes sweeping into view, in close proximity to the Settle and Carlisle Railway line. A train sped by on its way to Carlisle, passengers waving through the square windows as it passed. As they disappeared, I reciprocated their waves and felt the dreamlike sense of well-being that such brief, yet distant friendly human encounters invariably instil.

My expedition that afternoon was another of the Discover Eden walks: a route by the river to Lacy's Caves and then back to Little Salkeld via the stone circle known as Long Meg and Her Daughters. A disused signal box stands forgotten on the other side of the line. Once used to control a branch line from the Long Meg Gypsum Mine, it became obsolete when the mine closed in 1975. Gypsum deposits were formed all along the

Eden Valley when shallow lakes evaporated around 200 million years ago. The mine machinery was powered by steam and by a turbine in the river where the water runs rapidly over the weir. The remains of the mine are slowly being reclaimed by nature, as willow, birch and hazel scrub take hold. The path is hazardous in places where it gravitates closer to the river's precipitous bank and the dereliction of the mine workings gives way to mature woodland. I could almost smell the trees photosynthesising, their leaves absorbing the sunlight and filling the air with fresh, clean oxygen. As I took a long, deep breath, I was startled by the sudden screech of a jay protesting my impertinent appearance. It retreated to a darker part of the wood in erratic flight over my head, and I caught only a glimpse of its lovely pink and blue plumage.

I've walked this path on many occasions, yet I still experience the same thrill of anticipation as I approach the red outcrop of rocky sandstone ahead and glimpse the arched entrance to Lacy's Caves. The caves were excavated in a series of chambers by Lieutenant Colonel Samuel Lacy, the owner of Salkeld Hall in the eighteenth century, when it was fashionable to create romantic ruins and grottoes on country estates and pretend they were very old. They existed exclusively for his own and his guests' private amusement, as did the footpath. The path later became a Public Right of Way because it had subsequently been used by the miners who lived in nearby Kirkoswald and Lazonby, who walked back and forth along it every day.

The path goes over the roof of the caves and down to an area where the woods are being managed commercially with a crop of conifers. The ground along here is very wet, and the ECCP estate team used to visit regularly to dig drainage ditches, which promptly filled up with mud and silt as fast as they dug them. Inspired by recollections of a timber causeway I'd helped to construct across a peaty fen bog in an East Anglian National Nature Reserve and the generous quantities of Discover Eden Heritage Lottery money burning holes in my pockets, I had decided we would build a wooden boardwalk here. Ian Beale, ECCP's experienced and inventive estate team leader, supervised its assembly with all the creative panache of an Andy Goldsworthy.

Eight years on and three years after ECCP was closed down, it had suffered badly from a lack of routine maintenance and was ripped out by the river flooding its banks. Everywhere I go in the Eden Valley the sad demise of ECCP is all too apparent in the rapidly deteriorating condition of Public Rights of Way.

The path leaves the wood and leads into a field with an immediate and uninterrupted view of the river and Lazonby village beyond. There was another village here once called Addingham, which was washed away in the twelfth century when the river changed its course after a devastating flood. Several stone artefacts were retrieved from the riverbed in 1913 and taken to St Michael's church near Glassonby. I was heading that way and looking forward to seeing them, especially a tenth-century cross thought to have come from Addingham's drowned churchyard.

The parishes associated with Lazonby and Great Salkeld are examples of an area where landowners prevented paths being recorded on the Definitive Map. Lazonby and Salkeld parishes are both almost entirely bereft of public paths, and even two of the few endorsed by Lazonby Parish were prevented by an intransigent member of the landed gentry from crossing onto his property in Salkeld Parish. Consequently, a public footpath on the other side of the river from here and a public bridleway further over, near the railway, both terminate at the parish boundary.

Another of those ancient and neglected holy wells, called St Michaels Well, can be found in a field halfway between the two paths. It provided the inhabitants of Addingham with their drinking water and was the site of the original church. The path emerges at Daleraven Bridge, where Glassonby Beck has found its way into the Eden. The lane up to Glassonby is steep. Beneath it the earth is riddled with underground tunnels from the gypsum mine and therefore, as the road sign informs us, "liable to subsidence".

I turned off the lane onto a narrow-hedged track, which is a Byway Open to All Traffic (and wet enough in places to warrant being in a B.O.A.T!) The landowner uses this track to move live-stock safely from one field to another, and for pheasant rearing and forestry management. As an incidental by-product, it hosts a variety of habitats for wildlife.

The track divides into two routes, one going directly to Long Meg and Her Daughters and the other to St Michael's church. Why am I drawn to churches when they can make me feel so uncomfortable? Parts of this one are impressively old: the nave dates from the thirteenth century, and its chancel was built in 1512. The stone items collected from the river are kept in the porch and include a splendid Viking 'hogsback' tombstone. In the churchyard opposite stands the hammer-headed Anglian stone cross, designed as a rectangle with a hole in each corner; its surface is carved with a complex pattern of carved scrolling.

I enjoy walking along the bridleway from the church to Long Meg and Her Daughters because it affords such an enticing view of the stone circle from a distance. The circle consists of approx-imately sixty-five granite boulders. Some are huge and stand just as they did when their Neolithic builders first rolled them into place nearly five thousand years ago. Others are much smaller, and a few so insignificant that they are easily overlooked – per-haps the result of past attempts to bury them or break them up for building material. Colonel Lacy, the man who went to such trouble faking a sense of gothic antiquity with his caves, was behind a fortunately ill-fated attempt at the wholesale destruction, with explosives, of this ancient monument. No doubt he thought he could get away with it because many people believed such structures were the work of the devil. In the event, the men he'd sent to break up the stones were engulfed in a violent lightning and thunderstorm. They ran off in fright because they thought they'd incurred the wrath of evil spirits, angry at the prospect of the stone circle being destroyed.

Local scaremongering gave rise to the story of Long Meg and Her Daughters being witches turned into stone as a punishment for dancing on the Sabbath – and who will come back to life if anybody counts the same number of stones twice.

Long Meg herself is the tall pillar of red sandstone, decorated with faintly incised cup and ring spirals, that is set apart from the circle. Historians believe stone circles were constructed for religious purposes. They were certainly arranged with meticulous precision, usually in conjunction with the cycles of the sun and moon; Long Meg is perfectly aligned from the centre of the circle with the midwinter sunset. The middle of winter would have been a time of debilitating stress and deprivation in Neolithic times, and it is easy to imagine people there performing ceremonies and rituals that anticipated the return of summer.

Some people still carry out rituals and leave little offerings at the site; mostly these are trinkets and posies of flowers. Neopagans, Druids and motley other groups turn up every year to mark the winter solstice. One sleepy midsummers day I witnessed two women performing a wonderful T'ai Chi routine at the centre of the circle in graceful unison and with immaculate precision. Their trance-inducing elegance struck an apposite and powerful emotional chord in me. I remember how their intense concentration seemed to confer an exclusive, temporary

LONG MEG AND HER DAUGHTERS

ownership of the stones, and I slipped discreetly away. Ever since, when I visit the circle, a ghostly imprint of their dance comes to mind.

This time, I had the circle to myself and I stayed for quite a long while pondering the circularity of time: summer, autumn, winter and spring and the perpetual cycle of birth, life, death, birth, life, death ... just as the ancient architects of Long Meg and Her Daughters must have intended. I suppose stone circles are a kind of church, but I love their openness to the landscape and the sky and their direct relevance to nature and the wider world.

Eighteen

Swathes of Vermilion Red

Several weeks later I parked my car in the car park by Eden Bridge, just north of Lazonby village, where Frances Pelly's *Cypher Piece*, the sixth Eden Benchmark, is situated. Frances Pelly is a graduate of Duncan of Jordanstone College of Art and lives in Orkney. She divides her time between her own deeply personal work and public commissions, and almost everything she does is steeped in human history. Her residency was fraught with tension because she was anxious about being away from home so close to Christmas, but she nonetheless applied herself to the task in hand with determination.

I had found her a spacious workshop in the village where local people could visit as she worked. She was mostly left alone to develop her own ideas, but one exception was an elderly resident, born and bred in Lazonby, who arrived during her first week with a drawing he'd done of a dead horse. He explained that the location selected for the sculpture had once been a rubbish tip, and a horse pulling a cart full of rubbish to the site had fallen into the river and drowned. I think he expected Frances would carve a literally representational memorial of the unfortunate animal. Instead, she incorporated a stylised Celtic horse's head and just a hint, in the sculpture's slumping configuration, of a horse's recumbent body.

The sculpture sits on a raised mound of soil and is called *Cypher Piece* because it presents us with a series of puzzles to be decoded. The gap between the almost interlocking lumps of stone represents the river slicing through the landscape; a sun and moon have been carved at one end, and the variety of images elsewhere include a fish, 1996 in Roman numerals (MCMXCVI), a ram's horn and various decorative features copied from a Norse tomb. Little reminders of the history we can never repeat. But can we learn lessons from the past that will edify our management of the future?

We unveiled the sculpture during the early evening of December 21, 1996 to mark the winter solstice and lit a fire just as our ancestors might have done inside their stone circles. As we did so, a huge crystal ball moon levitated high in a lilac sky as the retreating sun flushed the horizon with swathes of vermilion red.

*   *   *

The River Eden revels in maturity at Lazonby, warranting the four striding arches of Eden Bridge to contain its expanding flow of water. I watched sand martins catching insects in the air above the river, dashing back and forth in front of the rows of dark holes in the riverbank opposite where the young were reared earlier in the summer.

A kilometre north of here is the picturesque village of Kirkoswald, its row of neat houses flanking a very steep main street. I stopped for half an hour in the cobbled market square listening to the comforting sound of rooks and jackdaws in the trees – the timeless soundtrack of an English village. Kirkoswald takes its name from the thirteenth-century church dedicated to St Oswald. Its belfry tower is quite separate on top of a hill just outside the village. Nearby there is a ruined castle and a grand set of buildings with the remains of a fortified Pele tower that was once a religious college. Once again, there is a close association between the church and a sacred well.

The Raven Beck comes through the lower end of Kirkoswald and joins the River Eden half a kilometre north of Eden Bridge.

Fed by sundry streams gathering on the precipitous fell above the remote hamlet of Renwick, it falls 457 metres in just over 6 kilometres and can be quite lively. Renwick used to be known for a rather more startling manifestation of local superstition than those lucky drinking cups: the occasional appearance of a terrifying creature combining the head, body and wings of a cockerel with the tail of a serpent, known as the Renwick Cockatrice. Thankfully, its last reported sighting was in 1973.

The fellside is embedded with features with names like Longtongue Beck, Skelling Moor, Hrafn Wic Fell and Beggaram Dun. *Hrafn* is Norse for raven, a forename adopted by the Vikings in deference to that clever member of the crow family, a bird both revered and feared by Nordic warriors. Odin, one of their most important gods, kept two ravens called Huginn and Muninn, meaning 'thought' and 'memory'. He regularly dispatched them to fly through the Vikings' fantasy nine worlds and bring back the latest gossip, uttered with corvine relish into his inquisitive ears.

Nineteen

'The Way Things Are Done Around Here'

Culture is all the information man possesses except that which is stored in the chemical language of his genes.

Dr Paul R. Ehrlich, in *The Population Bomb*

An important objective of the Discover Eden project was to explore the changes imposed on the physical landscape by human intervention. Certain factions in preservation circles, whose vision of the rural environment tends to be dominated by a sepia-tinged nostalgia for the parochial yesteryear of anachronistic country folk, refer to it as the cultural landscape. Ruminating on this notion got me thinking about what is meant by the word 'culture' in general, and it took me a while to work it out. Often confined to describing our recreational and social activities, it has in some contexts become virtually synonymous with the arts: it has evolved from simple systems of community communication to a modern phenomenon generated by a desire for individual self-expression. But culture in its widest sense is the traditional and habitual, deeply ingrained behaviour that people adhere to in their everyday lives. These are more obviously apparent in our observations of people from other countries than our own, but quite noticeable differences do exist, even today, from county to county in England, not to mention Scotland and Ireland. There is still a distinct residue of different cultures; different dialects, expressions and even languages, different food, different clothes, different ways of doing things.

A Cumbrian farmer might define culture as 'the way things are done around here', and that would be that – take it or leave it. A more useful definition differentiates between the hunger everyone feels when they wake up in the morning, which is a factor of biological survival, and the cultural preference of French people choosing to eat croissants and the English choosing fried eggs and bacon (assuming they are affluent enough to have the luxury of indulging any sort of preference). I'm not sure such a generalisation applies anymore; I sometimes have croissant for breakfast and I am regularly grateful for the fact that coffee, freshly ground from coffee beans rather than an instantly soluble powder, is now widely available in English cafés and no longer the separate cultural preserve of France and Italy as it was just a generation or so ago.

As for the influence of culture on the Cumbrian landscape, I'm not convinced of its significant or meaningful value in the twenty-first century when people are so much less provincial in their outlook and less prescriptive of 'how things should be done' in the countryside. Yet it has become a fashion in local government tourism propaganda and elsewhere to prioritise the influence of cultural diversity on sense of place, and the locally distinctive character of rural landscapes. Dry-stone walls in Cornwall and Devon are different in style from those in Yorkshire and Cumbria; hedge-laying techniques, where they still survive, vary from region to region; vernacular architecture, quite rightly, is lovingly preserved; cheeses and beers continue to reflect their geographical provenance as do different varieties of apples, breeds of sheep and cattle and the names of places.

These are all pleasing details, but I would argue that it is the topography, the geology of landscape and the flora and fauna associated with different parts of our countryside that matter more. Unfortunately, much of what we call culture is a breeding ground for human-centric attitudes that are often detrimental to landscape and increasingly and devastatingly damaging to wildlife.

During and after the foot and mouth epidemic in 2001 there were some vociferous and controversial discussions concerning the future viability of hill farming. It is frequently claimed that Cumbria's bare mountainous landscapes, made all the more bare by seventy years of subsidies for sheep grazing regimes, are the epitome of scenic perfection and a triumph of our cultural supremacy over nature. Some farmers insist that a creeping wasteland, as they see it, of impenetrable scrub, the outcome of a cessation of sheep farming, would be an unsightly affront to their good husbandry and proud rural traditions. But, on the contrary, it could ultimately rescue them from the futility of running in ever-decreasing circles in an increasingly impoverished desert of their own making.

These farmers are undermining the very life-support systems that could ensure their survival if only they could break free of their sheep-farming practices and return to an ecological mixed farming coexistence with nature. They don't need to be so aggressive in their subjugation of the more remote corners and isolated tracts of the landscape. Some seem to be driven by a culturally imposed 'waste not, want not' work ethic which has been exploited by misguided government financial incentives.

Much as I respect and admire hill farmers for their hard work, indefatigable determination against all the odds and the historically honourable status of their profession, I think the time has come to face up to the fact that collectively farmers have too many sheep on the hills. I believe this not merely from a simple economic perspective, but the incomparably more serious imperative of preventing a loss of wildlife diversity on a disastrous scale. Rather than fretting over the prospect of 'untidy' scrub that would grow as a consequence of fewer sheep grazing the slopes, it would represent a courageous acceptance that the subjugation of nature is ultimately self-defeating. Farmers might eventually come to recognise the benefits of allowing scrub to colonise the fells as a welcome precursor of the life-propagating ecosystems of mature woodland.

When farmers started to recover from the appalling impact of foot and mouth disease on their lives, it could have been an appropriate opportunity to take stock of the creeping changes in hill farming and the disconnection from a previously symbiotic relationship between farmers and the landscape. Six thousand years ago, before the arrival of pastoral and agricultural settlers, what we now call Cumbria was a land of unpolluted lakes and rivers, teeming with fish and surrounded by marsh and fen woodland; the lower slopes of the hills and mountains were covered with dense, high canopy woodland, supporting abundant populations of wild birds and animals, and the tops of the hills were alive with vast swards of heather and scrub. I'm not for a minute imagining that we can ever restore the original wilderness to its former glory, but surely with some rational environmental reassessment we could allow some moderate return of native woodland to the more remote margins of agricultural occupation.

Long before foot and mouth struck and the thousands of sheep and cattle were killed and burned, hill farming was already in decline and has only survived because the government and the European Union have given it massive financial support. Yet despite substantial subsidies, hill farmers continue to subsist on very meagre incomes, because the land and a changing climate tend not to be compatible with commercial agricultural enterprise.

The average age of a hill farmer is said to be approaching sixty years, and succeeding generations are less inclined to go on fighting this losing battle. Younger farmers have the advantage of a modern education and the capacity to combine a less environmentally corrosive approach to farming with a diverse range of alternative, but compatible, means of earning a living. Some of them even feel deeply uneasy about the damage they are doing to the natural world, but are trapped within a toxic matrix of ill-conceived government directives and what some see as bribery.

The ravages of foot and mouth disease denied public access to the countryside for almost a year and demonstrated that hill farming contributes less to the rural economy than tourism. Entrepreneurial hill farmers are already capitalising on the needs of our mainly urban population seeking regular respite from the pressures of city life. People crave affirmation of their rural roots: they want holidays in the countryside that enable them to dip into the process of food production at its source and see for themselves cows being milked, lambs being born and hens laying eggs. But they also expect to wake up to a dawn chorus of wild birds before eating a hearty breakfast of locally and humanely produced bacon and eggs and then going for a carefree walk to see carpets of wild flowers in flourishing, self-generating woodlands, along footpaths and bridleways and in hay meadows, before returning to go badger or deer watching in the evening.

More trees are now being planted. Two rewilding schemes in the Lake District, in which farmers in partnership with Natural England have agreed to remove sheep from the hills and plant thousands of native trees, are proving to be a great success. The flocks of sheep have readily adapted to grazing on lower ground closer to farmsteads and lowland pastures further afield.

Instead of propping up a rapacious but ailing sheep monoculture, the government could start by providing better financial incentives to conservation-minded farmers who are less stuck in their ways and willing to farm more sustainably, on a smaller, less wasteful scale. Other inducements would have to be more stringent, even compulsory, to ensure that millions more native trees are planted on fells and in gills on a massive scale and existing mature woodlands protected and allowed to regenerate and expand. We could relinquish the wettest places and allow them to be properly wet and marshy, or even transformed into lakes. They might even appease the strong brown river god and mitigate his propensity to flooding.

Twenty

At One with Nature

Just west of Staffield the road to Armathwaite crosses over Croglin Water, a short, energetic beck flowing down from the fells above Croglin village. It joins the River Eden in a sequence of waterfalls at the bottom of a deep gorge hidden away just beyond a large property called the Nunnery. Originally a Benedictine nunnery, parts of its walls are thirteenth-century, but most of the house was rebuilt between the sixteenth and nineteenth centuries.

When I first encountered the Nunnery, it was a hotel with a tea room open to the public. For a small fee, access was available through the gorge, potentially all the way down to the river, along ledges cut into the cliffs – although much of the route had become very dangerous. The path was well known for many years as the Nunnery Walks, and ECCP was involved with some restoration work to improve the routes in the gorge and make them safer, with a chain strung on metal posts (to hold onto for dear life) along the outer edge of the ledges. Now the Nunnery is a private house and the walks are no longer available to the public.

The tree-clad land on both sides of the river north of Kirkoswald, as far as Armathwaite, is another stretch of forbidden countryside where there are no public paths. Part of the reason is the prohibitive steepness of the red sandstone ravine, where much of the river is inaccessible to all but the most adventurous people in canoes, some intrepid climbers and the fee-paying fly fisherman who have exclusive and 'private ingress'. I turned into Coombs Wood at Longdales where there are brief glimpses of the river between the trees, before the ground levels and the trees thicken. I strolled down the wide track through a predominantly coniferous wood, planted and managed by the Forestry Commission for timber production. Tall stands of Scots pine give way to Douglas fir and Japanese larch. Although I prefer native broadleaved woods, a mature conifer plantation does have a welcome tranquillity, and I paused to enjoy the grandiose silence and the smell of resin pervading the air.

A solitary female roe deer sauntered onto the path some distance from where I was standing and hesitated, sniffing the air. There was not a breath of wind to transmit my scent in her direction, and she seemed confident that she had the woods to herself, proceeding to graze the vegetation along the edge of the path. I see roe deer almost everywhere in the Eden Valley, yet it is a constant surprise that such a large animal can hide so successfully in our busy countryside. The presence of red deer in parts of the Lake District is even more astonishing, as they are noticeably bigger. Of the six species of deer now living in the wild in Britain, red and roe are the only two natives. As I moved forward, the deer stared up at me and then, quite nonchalantly, crossed the path and disappeared from view.

A pheasant's cachinnation ricocheted briefly amongst the trees, and then a lovely silence prevailed. Halfway down the track the river comes into view again where two arcs of sandstone made up of nine large blocks straddle the path. One arc is carved with realistic representations of various items of clothing, a rucksack and a map. This is *Vista*, by Graeme Mitcheson, the seventh Eden Benchmark sculpture. The clothing includes walking boots, a sweater and a baseball cap, decorated with a plump little face, a reference to a series of mysterious and crudely chiselled faces on the cliff below that were allegedly carved by William Mounsey, the same man who made the original Jew Stone in

Mallerstang. The map functions as a sundial with a shadow cast by the upturned cuff of a strewn trouser leg.

The theme of the sculpture is being at one with nature; a lone walker has taken off his clothes and gone for a swim. Unfortunately, local people mindful of the walker's long absence have jokingly dubbed it the 'suicide stone'. Who knows, in centuries to come, what stories will be told about it. Graeme's grouping of several stones was inspirational, giving the carved stone a more inclusive and conceptual context as a focal point and meeting place at the centre of the wood.

The track continues through the woods and passes a well-worn, but unofficial, route down to the river where, if the level of the river isn't too high, it is possible to clamber along the base of the cliff to look at the carved faces. William Mounsey almost certainly chiselled out the crudely formed letters alongside the faces, in his own amended version of a verse from Izaak Walton's 'Compleat Angler':

Oh the fisher's gentle life
Happiest is of any;
Full of pleasure, void of strife…

He changed the third line to read "void of pleasure, full of strife", which suggests he didn't like fishing.

The official footpath re-joins the river just metres away, where conifers give way to deciduous woodland including some large beech trees. The river is noisy here as it passes over an old weir, but calms down again where Armathwaite village comes into sight. The path turns sharply away from the private garden surrounding Armathwaite Place and goes under Armathwaite Bridge to steps leading up to the road on the other side. There was no public access along this path until a few years ago, when the local parish council submitted evidence to Cumbria County Council that it had at one time been a public right of way and mistakenly omitted from the Definitive Map. Perhaps understandably, the landowner opposed the claim, but a government enquiry found in favour of the parish council's assertion.

Armathwaite is a handsome and expanding village with quite a few new houses, two good pubs, a grocery shop and a post office. The tiny church has two windows designed by Edward Burne-Jones, a prominent member of the mid-nineteenth century Pre-Raphaelite movement of painters. He was instrumental in a revival of interest in stained glass at the time.

Twenty-one

A Whisper of Fire
on its Breath

Weeks later, at the beginning of an unseasonably sweltering early September day, I walked from Armathwaite along the road parallel with the Settle and Carlisle Railway before turning right onto the lane past Drybeck Farm, beyond which there is a riverside footpath all the way to Wetheral. The river is huge here compared to the much narrower waterway I'm used to at Kirkby Stephen. I disturbed an assembly of waterfowl at a point where the river has gouged a secondary channel along the bank and created an island. Two herons, several cormorants, a family of startled mallard ducks and a pair of goosanders flew up from the shallow water as I approached.

Much of the ground along here is overgrown with the invasive Himalayan balsam. Introduced to Britain in 1839, it escaped from gardens all over the country and rapidly colonised riverbanks, suppressing or extinguishing all other plants in its seemingly unstoppable incursions. It's impenetrable and forces walkers progressively further away from the river. The purple-pink flowers first appear in June and later, when the seedpods mature, they explode to scatter the seeds, which not only take root in the immediate vicinity but also float down the river where they can survive for as long as two years, germinating in wet ground at any opportunity.

After a while, breaking free from the Himalayan balsam, its sweet, sickly smell accentuated by the heat of the midday sun, I followed the path up onto higher ground through remnants of cooler woodland. The path then emerges alongside the boundary of several fields, where a prominent red sandstone cliff called Hawkcliffe Scar, on the opposite bank, deflects the river westwards in a wide, shining sweep. The path climbs abruptly away, out of sight of the river, through mixed farmland, fields of cows and sheep, segmented with hedges and mature field boundary trees. One or two notices informed me that it is an organic farm, and the jays and nuthatches I heard calling indicated a farm in good heart.

At the end of the narrow wood I turned down to the river again, where the roar of its shallow water scrambling over rocks welcomed me back and then rewarded me with a brief glimpse of a kingfisher darting upstream in a straight line, a blur of orange and blue.

The heat was oppressive by the river, and the river seemed strangely bereft of wildlife. There were a few butterflies, mainly red admirals and peacocks, thriving in the warmth, but little else apart from a distant buzzard, which I saw gliding like Icarus across the face of the sun. I was relieved to immerse myself in the shade of the trees. A straggling mix has been planted alongside the river here, including beech, lime, cherry, horse chestnut and even a giant sequoia. A denser stand of woodland on the steeply ascending slope is called Edenbrows Wood. The Settle and Carlisle Railway runs 70 metres above the trees.

Some years after my walk, during a tempestuous December night, the riverbank collapsed, undermining the entire slope, and a half-million-tonne avalanche ripped the ground out from beneath the railway line. Storm Desmond had raged for three days and nights with gales and torrential rain causing havoc across Cumbria, flooding towns and villages and washing out bridges. The railway through Edenbrows Wood was closed for two years whilst a massive engineering project was implemented, involving two rows of concrete-filled steel tubes driven into the bedrock supporting a 1.5-metre-thick concrete slab as a base for the tracks. The riverbank has also been strengthened with drainage channels and heavy-duty revetment.

I tramped on past another island, Fishgarth Holm, where the main flow of the river continues on its far side, leaving a brackish, narrow, puddled stretch of backwater. My sudden arrival once again frightened a cohort of goosanders and cormorants, causing them to rise from the water in a spluttering frenzy. 'Garth' means an enclosed area, and the trapped, shallow water provides rich pickings for these clever fishing birds, hidden from the glare of human anglers. I'd passed several neatly mown areas of riverbank and fishermen's huts where large sums of money are paid for private fishing rights.

Two long fields of barley sit incongruously between yet more marauding Himalayan balsam screening the river and a plantation of dark conifers. The public footpath has given up the ghost here. The path is better accommodated further on through a pleasant open field opposite a neat farmhouse on the other side of the river.

I sat down on a fallen tree trunk for a much-needed rest. A cormorant flew past, and to my great delight in that same instant a dragonfly appeared, suspended in the warm air. Cormorants may have a primitive look about them, but dragonflies are truly primordial, with their unrivalled archaic credentials virtually unchanged in 300 million years. This particular one (I looked it up when I got home) was a southern hawker dragonfly. It shifted closer to my face as if to get a better look with its huge blue-green eyes. Then it turned away abruptly, its trembling silver wings and long black abdomen with lime green spots and pale blue stripes glittering in the sunshine. I watched as it resumed its flight along the riverbank and I fancied I could see a whisper of fire on its breath.

I am no dragonfly expert, but their take on mortality has always stuck vividly in my mind. Three hundred million years as a species, yet in our climate each individual dragonfly lives for three to five years as a clandestine larva, half-buried in murky silt at the bottom of a pond or slow-moving stream. Then, after its metamorphosis into an adult dragonfly, it has a short life expectancy of just a few months, feeding and breeding voraciously as if there might be no tomorrow.

This one probably metamorphosised from the depths of the ponds nearby, where abandoned claypits, once excavated for the manufacture of bricks, have gradually flooded and become surrounded with fen, scrub and woodland since a brickworks closed some years ago. There are four ponds fed by Pow Maughan Beck which flows 8 kilometres north from there to join a sinuous loop of the River Eden on the eastern agricultural fringe of Carlisle.

We need to save and restore our ponds. For centuries, ponds on village greens and farms throughout the land were an inherent part of Britain's rural character. Many farms had a pond in every field for the sheep and cattle to drink from. Village ponds were a convenient source of fish and provided drinking water for horses when they were the main means of transport and freight. Ponds were even used to wash carts and swell the wooden wheels to prevent the heavy iron rims falling off – as John Constable's much-loved painting *The Hay Wain* famously demonstrates. Ponds would have been muddy and trampled in those days, but there was always room for wildlife on the less accessible edges. Now that ponds are no longer needed for their original practical purposes, their potential wildlife value is still colossal. More than one thousand species of animals and insects can live in ponds.

Cote House Tower farmhouse comes into view where the path climbs away from the river opposite a third island. Built in the 1840s, the tower provided a vantage point from which the owners could look out for salmon poachers. The largest salmon ever caught in England have been caught in the River Eden, and up until the 1960s the Eden had England's finest run of spring salmon. In recent times there has been a decline due to excessive fishing at sea and pollution from agriculture.

The whole river and most of its tributaries were designated as a Site of Special Scientific Interest in 1997 and more recently, in a European context, a Special Area of Conservation because it contains habitats and species of wildlife that are rare or threatened throughout Europe.

After a gradual descent I was back by the river and into Wetheral Woods. Owned and managed by the National Trust, the woods support a variety of birds including, in the spring and summer, pied flycatchers, wood warblers and chiffchaffs. I stopped to listen to intermittent plops in the river, where fish were snatching flies from the surface before returning to their shady, sheltered depths.

Crossing a wooden bridge up some steps and over a second wooden bridge, I could see the small cave in the cliff high above the river known as St Constantine's Cells. The path goes above the cells, but you can visit them by turning right and forking back down a lower path that ends at the cells. Any connection with St Constantine has been lost in the mists of time, but Roman inscriptions in the vicinity may be evidence that excavation of the cells predates the Romans, who quarried stone from the cliff here for Hadrian's Wall. The cells were probably improved subsequently by the monks from Wetheral Priory, and it is likely that access to the cells was once only available by ladder, thus providing a secure hiding place for the monks and their valuables at times of danger. The soft sandstone has attracted much graffiti over the years, most notably three lines carved in 1852 by our old friend William Mounsey. His inscription is a quote in Old Welsh from the songs of Llywarch Hen, a Welsh poet of the early ninth century.

> *This leaf which is being persecuted by the wind,*
> *Let her beware of her fate.*
> *She is old though only born this year.*

Back up the steps I followed the lower path, keeping a wary eye on the steep slope down to the river. On the other side of the river there is an artificial island and some recently restored fish traps. These have replaced some that were originally built by the monks, who had exclusive rights to all the fish between here and the ford below Wetheral Viaduct.

I emerged from the woods through a kissing gate opposite the landscaped garden of Corby Castle, which was laid out in the eighteenth century by Thomas Howard. The impressive cascade falls 30 metres to a basin where there used to be a fountain. Corby Castle is not much like a castle now, but a wooden castle here dating from the eleventh century was replaced by a stone Pele tower in the thirteenth century. Henry Howard completely remodelled the castle in 1812, creating the classical façade we can see today that hides the Pele tower. The stone walkway along the bank below was added by a more recent owner.

Wetheral Viaduct is a commanding presence across the river. Built between 1830 and 1834, it carries the Carlisle to Newcastle railway and provides a footway between Wetheral and Great Corby. A rowing boat ferry was available here until the middle of the 1950s. The ferryman lived in the cottage opposite.

A WHISPER OF FIRE ON ITS BREATH

* * *

The eighth Eden Benchmark sculpture, *Flight of Fancy*, is a welcome sight. The sculptor who made it is Tim Shutter, whose site-specific sculptures at many locations throughout Britain include a variety of similarly comfortable-looking stone seats. He is a master stonemason trained in the classical tradition and he is known for his superlative carving skills.

Influenced by St Constantine's Cell, St Columba's Well and the nearby Wetheral Church, Tim applied ecclesiastical notions of lifting the spirit with angel's wings, church-style masonry and some convincing carved prayer cushions. The low, horizontal line of the sculpture, with its depiction of the viaduct on the back, harmonises with the flatness of the river and reinforces a visual sense of flying up the bank opposite.

Made with St Bees sandstone, it is regularly submerged by the river in flood and looks as though it has been there for hundreds of years. I did mention to Tim that several local people had expressed their reservations about siting it too close to the river's edge, where flooding would regularly subject it to a soaking, but he seemed to welcome the prospect as being part of his concept.

Wetheral village was once a hub of busy farming activity, with goats, pigs and geese as well as sheep grazing the village green, and a communal water supply in constant use in the corner by the three pillars. The word *wether* is Anglo-Saxon for a castrated male sheep; it is still used to this day. Villagers would also have spent much of their leisure time here, and a maypole once stood where the stone cross is now situated.

Twenty-two

Gelt, the Magic River

The call of the curlew is my call, the tremble of the harebell is my tremble in life. The blue mist of the lonely fells is my mystery and the silver gleam when the sun does come out is my pathway.

Winifred Nicholson, in *Unknown Colour*,
edited by Andrew Nicholson

There are almost no public paths adjacent to the River Eden between Wetheral and the area east of Carlisle, so during the course of the next few weeks I resorted to a succession of car journeys and a few short walks in the wider vicinity.

Just north of Warwick Bridge the Eden is joined by the River Irthing, flowing down from the Scottish border north of Gilsland, where it divides Cumbria from Northumberland. The wild-wooded Irthing Gorge at Gilsland is managed by the Woodland Trust. There is a large rounded stone in the gorge where Sir Walter Scott proposed marriage to Charlotte Charpentier. The river winds its way from there south-west and parallel with Hadrian's Wall past Lanercost Priory, a twelfth-century monastery founded by Augustinian monks under the patronage of Robert de Vaux, Lord of Gilsland. It is now a picturesque, well-preserved ruin, although part of it has been restored as the parish church. In the north aisle there are three stained glass windows designed by Edward Burne-Jones. Behind the altar is a banner of embroidered cloth known as *The Lanercost Dossal*, commissioned in 1881 by George Howard, the ninth Earl of

Carlisle. Designed by William Morris, the Dossal was made by women of the parish.

George Howard's granddaughter, the distinguished artist Winifred Nicholson, lived for many years at Bankshead, close to Hadrian's Wall, until her death in 1981. After her divorce from Ben Nicholson she concentrated on painting exquisite pictures of flowers arranged in vases and jugs, often placed on windowsills, with the outside landscape of Tindale Fell and the Pennine hills behind her garden as a backdrop. She developed a style using intense colours, and Kathleen Raine, a close friend, described her as an artist "of rare truth who saw the poetry in flowers". Somehow, she captured the unseen colours either side of the visible spectrum and filled her paintings with radiant light. Tate Britain owns several of her most eloquent paintings, and in 2016 one of her landscapes of St Ives Harbour in Cornwall was sold at a Sotheby's auction for £200,000.

* * *

The Irthing has its own tributaries, notably King Water and the River Gelt, but whereas King Water originates from the same fells as the Irthing, the River Gelt has its source in the Pennines above Castle Carrock. The Gelt is a river with great character; the name may derive from an Irish word meaning 'wild', brought to the area by migrating Norse settlers, or it could also be a variation of the Gaelic word *galt*, meaning 'magic'. Rising in the Pennines above Castle Carrock, there is something about the River Gelt's journey through this rocky landscape that is both wild and magical. I got to know it a little when I devised a walk route for the Discover Eden series of booklets, focussing mainly on the woods surrounding the river.

On a return visit I followed some of that same route and walked along a track known as Thief Street, allegedly used five hundred years ago as an escape route by the Border Reivers hiding stolen cattle in the woods. *Reive* is an old dialect word meaning 'to plunder'. The Reivers were the mafia of their day and, as well as rustling cattle and raiding and burning homesteads, they operated vicious protection rackets. Emanating from a relatively small area of no-man's land at the western end of the Border that was known at the time as the debatable land, they expanded their reign of terror over a wide region of the Border country. Their lawless lifestyle continued for some three hundred years. The perpetrators belonged to more than two hundred different families, who were so violent in pursuit of their ruthless regime that they terrorised, robbed and killed one other as well as their more law-abiding neighbours. It has been suggested that the word 'bereaved' came from 'be-reived' because a visit from the Reivers invariably left at least one of their victims dead. The word 'blackmail' also originates from that time; *greenmayle* was the rent paid during the day by tenant farmers for agricultural land and *blackmayle* was the protection money collected by the Reivers at night.

Most of the woodland in the vicinity of the River Gelt has been designated a Site of Special Scientific Interest. The woods are an important example of gorge woodland of a type peculiar to northern Cumbria and parts of Scotland, with a rich mix of native trees including sessile oak, hairy and silver birch, rowan, holly and hazel. Some areas were clear felled after the Second World War and planted up with larch, Scots pine and other conifers.

Part of the wood has been managed by the Royal Society for the Protection of Birds. Forty years ago, the original native trees were felled in large parts of Gelt Woods and replaced with conifers to provide a quick growing crop of timber. The RSPB gradually removed them to facilitate a naturally regenerated return to native woodland more compatible with indigenous wildlife. Some scrub has been encouraged to provide a habitat for summer migrant birds including the chiffchaff and garden warbler, and shallow pools have been dug out in the wet ground for frogs and toads.

A spectacular cliff face in the middle of the wood is the result of an old quarry, excavated over several centuries, first by the Romans and more recently by local people who had commoners' rights to quarry here in what was once the Brampton Freestone Quarry. Many of the buildings in Brampton were constructed with stone extracted from the Gelt Woods area.

There is a stone and timber seat, commissioned by Iris Glimmerveen who was the woodlands officer at ECCP, tucked away in front of the cliff, made by the sculptor Vivien Mousdell. The text on the seat is taken from an ancient Chinese Taoist manuscript comparing the human journey through life with that of a river through a rocky landscape.

Soft yielding water overcomes the hard rock
Low flowing river overcomes the high crag.

Powterneth Beck runs into the River Gelt here, which continues for 3 kilometres to the west before joining the River Irthing.

*   *   *

In the car park a pair of crows lacerated the air with rasping croaks that sound to some like carping notes of discontent. Much disliked by country people, carrion crows excite an animosity every bit as anthropomorphic as my *Wind in the Willows* sentimentality. Crows, rooks, jackdaws, hawks, weasels, stoats, foxes and badgers all suffer the dire consequences of people confusing a carnivorous wild animal's instincts to avoid starvation with their own deeply ingrained human desire to plunder, torture and kill for pleasure. I often hear people describing a fox's occasionally frantic slaughtering antics in a chicken coup as being 'a wicked act of killing for the sake of killing' when, in fact, it is an opportunistic, instinctive response to an artificial situation. If people who keep chickens made sure their chicken enclosures were fox-proof, then the fox would look elsewhere for its dinner. Breeders of pheasants who choose for their shooting pleasure to fill pens in woods with unnaturally large numbers of young birds should also construct stronger, predator-proof pens. Do they really expect the predatory wild creatures they think of as vermin to have the ability to discriminate between ground-skulking birds put there by a gamekeeper and those that turn up naturally? Even some well-known wildlife writers persist in describing the scattered and bloodied feathers of a bird killed by a sparrowhawk as evidence of a 'crime scene' and the perpetrator 'murderous'. Sparrowhawks and other predatory birds and mammals hunt to eat, fundamentally in order to survive.

Twenty-three

Carlisle

Winter was looming when I resumed my journey in Carlisle, crossing the memorial footbridge into Rickerby Park where the River Petteril joins the Eden. Carlisle has an admirable collection of parks that are like an oasis of countryside in the middle of the city.

The River Petteril begins at Motherby, 8 kilometres west of Penrith, travelling north past Greystoke and meandering east via Newton Reigny and under the M6 before turning north again just 3 kilometres north of Penrith, between the motorway and the A6. An artificial watercourse called Thacka Beck runs from there to Penrith where it is conveyed, mainly underground, to discharge into the River Eamont near Carleton. It was excavated at the instigation of a priest called William Strickland in 1382, who later became a Bishop of Carlisle, to provide the residents of Penrith with a regular supply of fresh water.

The Petteril continues its journey to Carlisle between the M6 and the West Coast mainline railway through Southwaite and east of Wreay, where there is a very attractive and unusual church. Built in the early nineteenth century, it was designed and financed by a remarkable, fiercely independent local woman called Sara Losh. Born in 1785, she was the highly educated daughter of a wealthy businessman and farmer who died young, leaving her his entire estate. She travelled extensively on the continent and was so influenced by the architecture in Italy that she decided to become an architect herself.

Her church in Wreay was completed in 1842 and is an extraordinary forerunner of the Arts and Crafts Movement, which emerged forty years later when William Morris initiated a revival of artisan craft skills in defiance of the mass production methods of the Industrial Revolution. She based her design on the early Italian churches she admired, but adapted the style to resemble Cumberland vernacular with contemporary originality. The outside of the church is plain, almost severe, but decorated below the eaves with gargoyles representing a turtle, a tortoise, a crocodile, a snake and a dragon. The doors and windows are embellished with carvings of natural forms such as ammonites, birds, insects and vegetation. The church interior is an Aladdin's cave of ornamental artwork in wood, glass and stone, most of it made by local craftsmen and depicting a wonderful medley of images including fossils, pine cones, animals and flowers. Sara Losh herself carved an alabaster font full of floating lotus flowers and leaves. She was a feminist, far ahead of her time, who deserves to be much better known. Her church, which seems to embrace all religions and none, is a wonderful manifestation of the radical, visionary depth of her philosophical interpretation of life, death and constant renewal in nature. Here was a church where I found great comfort.

The Petteril flows through Wreay Woods where a public footpath provides some welcome access. The woods are owned by Carlisle City Council and managed as a nature reserve by Cumbria Wildlife Trust. The public footpath then continues all the way into Carlisle from there.

* * *

I crossed over the Eden again on the road bridge and walked along the riverbank to Bitts Park. The Eden's last main tributary, the River Caldew, makes its dramatic entrance here. The Petteril's larger sibling emanates from the eastern slopes of Skiddaw, one of the highest mountains in the Lake District National Park. It flows north, near Hesket Newmarket and Caldbeck, through Buckabank after collecting the River Roe on its way, then east of Dalston and into the city through Denton Holme. There is good public access along the northern section of the Caldew, notably the Cumbria Way from Caldbeck.

A weir close to where the Caldew joins the Eden was recently removed by the Eden Rivers Trust as part of the River Eden Restoration Strategy, which aims to return Eden catchment rivers to a more natural state. The strategy includes reinstating twists and turns where rivers have been straightened in the past, reducing pollution from farm slurry and phosphate fertiliser, and removing the man-made barriers that prevent salmon, trout and other fish from migrating up and down rivers to breed. Weirs were mainly built to facilitate mills, which are now redundant, and the Eden Rivers Trust has identified more than two hundred weirs and other barriers it hopes to remove or modify.

Much of the river restoration work will also help to reduce flooding. Carlisle was devastated by floods in 2005, and the Environment Agency has since spent £38 million on a flood alleviation scheme. It adopted a propitiously comprehensive approach by combining flood abatement measures with riverside cycle ways, footpaths and bridges as well as improving wildlife habitats. The Agency worked closely with local residents to ensure that the appearance of the flood defences harmonised with the landscape and a small team of first-rate artists were commissioned to help them do it. A riverside art trail incorporates forty decorative, brightly coloured enamel plaques depicting images pertinent to Carlisle and its three rivers.

The ninth Eden Benchmark sculpture is located alongside the River Eden in Bitts Park. This is *Toward the Sea,* by Hideo Furuta. The four components of this exceptional sculpture are manifestations of the sculptor's intense, mathematical explorations of stone. They depict the gradual emergence of a sphere from inside a cube in a sequence descriptive of water-eroded stone running parallel with the flow of the river, a geometrical evocation of gestation and procreation. The carving skills involved are astounding.

Hideo Furuta died in 2007 at only fifty-seven years of age. An artist of international standing, based in his last years at a granite quarry near Creetown, Galloway, he was the subject of a television documentary in 1997 called *Moving Mountains*. Born in Hiroshima four years after America dropped the atomic bomb, he studied art and philosophy in Tokyo before training as a stonemason and quarryman. He settled in Scotland in 1989 after a sculpture residency in Edinburgh, where he also studied contemporary classical music as a percussionist. He described his own musical compositions as "sculpture to be listened to," with titles like *Unity, Breathing and Quiescence,* and organised student seminars to explore the relationships between science, visual art and music. A gentle and charming man, he is remembered with great affection by everyone who knew him.

Carlisle has a turbulent history. Fought over by the Scots and English for centuries, the city still seems to have an air of post-traumatic stress about it. The castle is a grim reminder of all the appalling conflict and horror. My blood runs cold when I think about the so called 'licking stone', set in a dungeon wall once wet with damp, where scooped-out depressions still remain, worn down by the rasping tongues of desperate prisoners deprived of water and left to die.

The castle is separated from the main part of the city by a busy dual carriageway, and a subway is provided for pedestrians. The subway contains a striking reminder of the Reivers – hidden, appropriately, underground. Commissioned by Carlisle City Council as a Millennium project in 2001, the *Bishop's Stone* was devised by artist Gordon Young and designer Andy Altman. Set on a granite floor bearing the names of Reiver families, it is a 7.5-tonne polished granite boulder inscribed with an excerpt from a much longer, ranting curse issued against the Reivers in 1525 by Gavin Dunbar, Archbishop of Glasgow. Part of it reads:

> *I curse thair heid and all the haris of thair heid; I curse thair face, thair ene, thair mouth, thare neise, thair toung, thair teith, thair crag, thair schuderis, thair breast, thair hert, thair stomok, thair bak, thair wame, thair armes, thair leggis, thair handis, thair feit, and everilk part of thair body, frae the top of thair heid to the soill of thair feit, befoir and behind, within and without.*

It was known as the 'Monition of Cursing', and the bishop instructed that it should be proclaimed from every pulpit in the Diocese and circulated the length and breadth of the Border region. The Reivers, however, carried on with their violent ways for many more years to come and took no more notice of this threat of divine intervention than they did the human laws of the land.

A strange postscript to this in our own time was the reaction of a number of superstitious people after the stone was installed. They included a modern-day archbishop and local church clergy who in all seriousness blamed the cursing stone for foot and mouth disease as well as the floods in the city and demanded its removal and destruction. Fortunately, Carlisle city councillors voted to keep the stone. A rational, even indifferent, assent has prevailed ever since.

The city has a splendid cathedral. Constructed in the early twelfth century, the building has endured all the usual catastrophes and misfortunes. Severely damaged by fire in 1292 and partly demolished in the Civil War by Scottish Roundheads who used the stone to reinforce the structure of Carlisle Castle, it has been extensively repaired and refurbished. Certain important early features have survived, and visitors can still enjoy the visual splendour of the original medieval stained-glass east window, constructed soon after the fire in 1350. The roofing timbers date from 1400, but the strikingly attractive star-studded blue ceiling was designed in 1853 by a prominent decorative artist called Owen Jones. Sir Walter Scott was married in this cathedral on Christmas Eve in 1797. The building as a whole constitutes a powerful affirmation of Christian resilience and must surely embody, for those who need it, an antidote to that innocuous underpass boulder.

Sitting outside a café near the cathedral, I watched groups of pigeons and starlings searching for scraps of food. Starlings are remarkable birds. Stocky and brazen, they pace the city pavements and squares searching for food dropped by humans, their plumage glossy with a green, blue and purple sheen. They mix their own harsh and rattling voices with impersonations of other birds. In rural areas, as spring approaches, they imitate the call of a curlew, whereas starlings in the city excel at copying the sounds of telephones, vehicle alarms and police-car sirens.

Nightly retirement in the city to comfortable ledges on convenient buildings is preceded by the lengthy and spellbinding spectacle known as a murmuration, when small groups congregate at dusk, flying in from all directions as if responding to some predetermined instruction. Gradually amalgamating to form an ever-expanding, closely packed multitude, they move in perfect harmony through the air as one large, fluid, shape-shifting collective mass. They glide and soar as the light recedes, audibly whooshing by with the effortless precision of a choreographed aerial dance, before suddenly dispersing and making their way to their chosen buildings.

Twenty-four

Global Warming

Man is part of nature and his war against nature is inevitably a war against himself.

From *Silent Spring*, by Rachel Carson

I was impatient by now to conclude what had become a very long drawn-out journey over two or three years, instead of the one year I'd planned at the outset. Frustratingly, a bout of ill health prevented me from walking the last stretch of the river from Carlisle to the village of Rockcliffe so, desperate to finish, I resorted again to my car. Autumn had come and gone, and winter was underway.

I had walked the penultimate leg of the Eden journey before. It was a bit of a slog, mostly spent escaping what seemed to be the inextricable sprawling expansion of Carlisle.

I can't remember seeing much of interest, although I do rec-ollect two disparate observations. One was the life-affirming recurrence of blue damselflies locked together in mating pairs around the water-washed roots along a row of alder trees. The other was a shocking accumulation of plastic – bottles, packaging and bags – scattered across the fields beside the river. Alternately deposited and picked up again at regular intervals by the fall and rise of the river, plastic is all too quickly carried out to sea and the oceans beyond.

The last Eden Benchmark sculpture is located at Rockcliffe, carved from a block of red sandstone by the Devon-based sculp-tor Anthony Turner. On the morning of its unveiling I arrived early to find him chiselling its curved surface with a perfection-ist's last-minute flourishes. An intensely thoughtful man with a wry sense of humour, he made me laugh, even after his depar-ture, when I discovered a tiny pyramid of sandstone he'd placed, with meticulous care in the middle of the otherwise scrupulously swept workshop floor. I have it at home on a shelf, and it still makes me smile all these years later.

But the sculpture at Rockcliffe is a serious expression of his apprehension about the deteriorating health of our planet. Situated below a red sandstone cliff, where the River Eden slides ever closer to the sea, it projects an expanding awareness of the wider world. It could simply represent a huge sea creature washed upstream and onto the riverbank, but its resemblance to the planet Earth held carefully in the palm of a human hand con-veys the sense of an even bigger, universal scale. Anthony called it *Global Warming*.

Average temperatures are escalating at twice the rate they were fifty years ago, primarily due to the gargantuan quantities of carbon dioxide being released into the atmosphere by our insa-tiable combustion of fossil fuels. The worldwide loss of forests, which would otherwise store carbon, massively exacerbates the problem. Other causes are heat-retaining gases, such as methane from landfill sites and the digestive systems of cattle, and nitrous oxide produced from the manufacture of fertiliser. Ice is melting in both polar regions; as the ice melts, so sea levels rise. Soon this could mean that coastal areas where half the world's human population lives become submerged. The effects of global warm-ing on the earth's ecosystems will be catastrophic as extreme weather conditions play havoc with seasonal processes and devas-tate wildlife habitats. Entire species are dying out at an appalling rate, and Britain is no exception, as we are now one of the most nature-depleted countries in the world.

GLOBAL WARMING

Yet sitting on the Rockcliffe sculpture that particular morning it was easy just to close my eyes in an interlude of denial and bask in the more congenial global warming of some very welcome winter sunshine.

*   *   *

From Rockcliffe I walked alongside the final stretch of the river, anticipating a glimpse of the Solway estuary ahead. As I did so a skein of geese materialised high in the sky, passing through thin shrouds of cloud in a ragged V-shaped formation, wings lifting and descending, each bird riding on the air from underneath the wings of the bird in front. Geese take it in turns being leader and share the job of generating a slipstream to reduce the effort of their graceful flight. I wasn't sure if they were greylag, pink-footed or barnacle geese and blamed my ignorance on the clouds obscuring my view.

I continued as far as I dared. The public footpath terminates just short of the vast expanse of Rockcliffe Marsh, where the Eden cuts a channel through tidal deposits of mud and sand, heading for the sea and the distant oceans. Five kilometres north from here, on the far side of the marsh, the River Esk, emerging from Scotland, does likewise with a few meanders along the coast just south of Gretna.

Protectively embraced by the wide, saturated, muddy margins of both rivers, the grass and sedge mosaic of the marsh reaches out to the sand-shifting estuarine wilderness beyond, providing thousands of wading birds, like turnstone, godwit and dunlin, with a safe and rich feeding ground. In the winter months the marsh is of particular importance as a major refuge for the barnacle geese that migrate here to escape the freezing temperatures of Spitsbergen in northern Norway, where they breed in the warmer summers. A significant proportion of these attractive geese, as well as the other breeds of geese and swans, are looked after by the Wildfowl and Wetlands Trust at Caerlaverock, on the Scottish side of the Solway. Thanks to the committed effort of nature conservationists, most of the Solway is officially a nature sanctuary, and the population of barnacle geese has gradually increased from an endangered 300 in the 1940s to a very healthy 35,000 today. The marsh is also grazed by sheep and cattle, and the grazing regime is carefully managed to accommodate the geese, with the generous cooperation of the farmers concerned.

I stood like a child peeping over the sill of a high window, looking out at the tantalising striated green and glistening brown wonderland in front of me. Public access on the marsh is prohibited, to avoid disturbing the wildlife and also because it can be dangerous. The ebb and flow of fast tides, treacherous currents, quicksand and steep-sided creeks all conspire against the safe passage of ignorant or inept human walkers. Both of these categories certainly apply to me, and I didn't want to end up face down in a saltwater-filled creek. So, I turned away, resolving to visit Caerlaverock next winter to watch the wildlife from the safe, comfortable vantage point of a bird hide – and hopefully learn more about identifying geese in flight.

Wild geese have a unique and charismatic presence in the sky. They take possession of it with an effortless confidence in the strength of their flight. Celtic people revered them as manifestations of human souls, restlessly traversing the unfathomable firmament in conjunction with the cycles and seasons of their ceaseless migrations.

The autumn appearance of barnacle geese over the Solway remained a mystery for centuries. Their name comes from a long-held belief that they emerged from molluscs below the sea, which were then washed ashore attached to driftwood. Like

Botticelli's *The Birth of Venus,* they were believed to rise from shells on the seashore.

The reality of their beginning, however, is far from romantic. The day-old flightless chicks, freshly hatched from eggs laid at the top of high, inland rocky cliffs, are obliged to throw themselves over the edge, their little bodies plunging down, bouncing, if they are lucky, from ledge to ledge, and crashing onto grassy ground far below, where they can graze. Those that survive predation build up their strength as adults through the Arctic summer months in preparation for their winter migration.

On arrival here they find a well-deserved safe haven in this vast, polymorphic, waterlogged morass where the accelerating stream of the River Eden is rapidly consumed by the powerful tides of the Irish Sea.

Afterword

My journey along the River Eden has been an absorbing and sometimes enthralling experience. I'm not a botanist, an ornithologist, an entomologist or a zoologist. I've enjoyed watching wildlife all my life, on a laissez-faire basis, as a pleasant accompaniment to my work in habitat and countryside management. The River Eden catchment is a scenic paradise and I have rejoiced in its beauty. Some of the wildlife that kept me company as I roamed that same scenic paradise twenty years ago, however, seems to be in trouble. There are fewer birds, fewer mammals, fewer reptiles, fewer insects and fewer wildflowers – even in paradise.

Wildlife is disappearing everywhere. We are perilously close to the brink of an irreversible ecological Armageddon. Our children and our children's children should be made aware that, as well as having so much in common with the birds and bees where procreation is concerned, we are also part of the same natural scheme of things. Humanity isn't separate: we are an integral component of the natural world, and within that context, as rational thinking humans we have the unique extra intellectual power to organise and maintain an equitable natural balance. In Britain the recent implementation of alternative technologies including solar, wind and geothermal systems have initiated some improvement, but we need to do so much more.

The birds and bees sustain our planet. If birds and bees are facing extinction, then so are we. It's taken us more than fifty years of carelessly discarding plastic to realise that plastic waste has been increasingly, silently running riot in our oceans. More than five trillion pieces of plastic, collectively weighing 269,000 tonnes, are floating on the surface of our seas. And there are trillions more below the surface. Over time the plastic breaks down into tiny particles that are ingested by fish, and in turn by us when we eat the fish. And, lest we forget, plastic is made in the first place from petrochemicals, the production of which is also a major contributor to global warming.

There are, of course, some good things happening in the world, and wonderful people fighting a good fight to safeguard and cherish the natural environment and perpetuate our miraculous wild places. The barnacle geese on the Solway marsh are an admirable example of what can be achieved. Propitious conservation measures fifty years ago saved otters and peregrine falcons from extinction. But nature conservationists and natural habitats are under siege like never before. Misguided or self-serving politicians and gangster-style dictators with egocentric, short-term agendas are taking us ever closer to mass planet destruction.

Most of us love the buzzing of bees and the virtuosic flight and music of birds. Yet so many of us feel helpless, despite knowing full well we are destroying Earth's biodiversity and wildlife. I still have a modicum of hope that political indifference to the natural environment can be overcome if enough of us who care shout loud enough in defence of our precious blue and green planet and its irreplaceable flora and fauna. But we are running out of time.

Acknowledgements

My main thanks must go to my partner Sue for her patience, fortitude and pragmatism in support of my writing journey, with all its up and downs, and my frequent loss of confidence as a somewhat self-indulgent journal, written for my private gratification, slowly emerged as a possible candidate for publication.

The first hint of this crept in when I joined a writing group led by Vicki Bertram, to whom I owe a heartfelt debt of gratitude for her generous encouragement, with just the right balance of critical and helpful analysis. I'd also like to thank other members of the group, including Karen Babayan, not least for her moral support when my self-esteem frequently faltered; Sarah Kirkup; Clare Hallam; Sue Haywood; and David and Barbara Haigh.

My thanks also to Barbara Dowson, proprietor of Kirkby Stephen's bookshop, who suggested I seek advice from freelance editor Charlotte Cole who, in turn, reiterated Vicki's opinion that my manuscript had the makings of a proper book. She also recommended sending my manuscript to Saraband.

Sara Hunt at Saraband has been wonderful beyond belief! Having promptly and generously approved and accepted my manuscript she then, with considerable kindness and patience, helped me knock it into better shape in conjunction with some very proficient editing and proofreading by her hard-working colleagues.

Last but not least I'd like to thank Andrew Forteath for his powerful design on the book's cover and photographers Val Corbett, Barry Stacey and John Stock for allowing me to include their wonderful pictures.

Publisher's note

The publisher would like to thank Meg Peacocke for granting permission for the reproduction of her poems in this book, as well as Aisling Holling and Lauren Brooke for proofreading.